SHE RISES

SHE LEADS, SHE LIVES

OVERCOMING OBSTACLES
AND THRIVING AGAINST ALL ODDS

HANNA OLIVAS

ALONG WITH 23 INSPIRING AUTHORS

TABLE OF CONTENTS

INTRODUCTION

Welcome to *She Rises, She Leads, She Lives: Overcoming Obstacles and Thriving Against All Odds*. In this collection of powerful stories, you'll meet women who have faced life's harshest challenges and emerged not just unbroken, but triumphant. This is not a book of simple victories, but a celebration of the grit, courage, and strength that lies beneath every woman's journey—no matter how different her path may be.

Here, you will find intimate portraits of women who have stared down adversity with unwavering determination. Some have battled personal loss, others have defied societal expectations, and many have overcome obstacles that seemed insurmountable. But each one of them has something in common: they didn't just survive—they thrived.

These are stories of resilience, resourcefulness, and the incredible power of the human spirit. They invite you into the hearts and minds of women who, in the face of hardship, found a way to rise—not for the applause, but for themselves. Their courage is not defined by the absence of fear or pain, but by the act of moving forward despite it.

As you journey through these pages, you'll witness profound insights, unexpected twists, and moments of raw emotion. You'll encounter not just stories of struggle, but stories of wisdom, transformation, and empowerment. The women in these pages offer more than just inspiration—they offer the kind of lived wisdom that can change your perspective, ignite your own inner strength, and remind you that, no matter the odds, you too have the power to rise.

In a world that often seeks to limit or define women by external forces, these stories will show you that the truest power comes from within. *She Rises, She Leads, She Lives* is a tribute to every woman who has ever faced down adversity and emerged with a deeper sense of purpose, strength, and vitality. This book is for every woman who is still rising, still leading, still living.

Hanna Olivas

Founder and CEO of SHE RISES STUDIOS

https://www.linkedin.com/company/she-rises-studios/
https://www.facebook.com/sherisesstudios
https://www.instagram.com/sherisesstudios_llc/
www.SheRisesStudios.com

Author, Speaker, and Founder. Hanna was born and raised in Las Vegas, Nevada, and has paved her way to becoming one of the most influential women of 2022. Hanna is the co-founder of She Rises Studios and the founder of the Brave & Beautiful Blood Cancer Foundation. Her journey started in 2017 when she was first diagnosed with Multiple Myeloma, an incurable blood cancer. Now more than ever, her focus is to empower other women to become leaders because The Future is Female. She is currently traveling and speaking publicly to women to educate them on entrepreneurship, leadership, and owning the female power within.

She Rises. She Leads. She Lives.

By Hanna Olivas

In the dim light of the bathroom, the steam from the shower enveloped me like a cocoon. It was a moment of clarity amidst the chaos of my life. My world had been turned upside down with the weight of my recent diagnosis—cancer. The news hung heavily over me, like a dark cloud threatening to obscure the light of hope. Yet, in that moment, as the warm water cascaded over me, three simple yet profound words echoed through my mind: She rises. She leads. She lives.

These words resonated deep within my soul, weaving through the fabric of my existence. They were not merely phrases; they were a mantra—a call to action that transcended my diagnosis, my fears, and the uncertainties that lay ahead. I knew then that this journey, however daunting, was not just about surviving. It was about thriving, embracing my power, and living fully in the face of adversity.

She Rises

To say she rises is to acknowledge the strength that lies within every woman. Rising is not simply about getting out of bed in the morning; it is about the courage to face each day with resilience and determination. It is about rising above challenges, fears, and the doubts that seek to weigh us down.

When I think of rising, I think of the phoenix—a symbol of rebirth and renewal. In my life, I had experienced my share of challenges: the trials of motherhood, the struggles of entrepreneurship, and now, the battle against cancer. Each of these experiences could have served to break me, but instead, they became the very foundation upon which I built my strength.

There were days when the weight of my diagnosis felt unbearable. I would lie in bed, consumed by fear and uncertainty. Yet, in those moments, I remembered the power of rising. I would take a deep breath, close my eyes, and visualize myself standing tall, unyielding against the storm. "I rise," I would whisper to myself, drawing on the strength of every woman who had come before me—those who had faced their own battles and emerged victorious.

Rising means acknowledging our pain and using it as fuel for our journey. It means surrounding ourselves with love and support, allowing those who care for us to lift us when we cannot stand on our own. "Sometimes you need to take a leap of faith first. The trust part comes later," I remind myself, recalling the wisdom of Maya Angelou. With each challenge I faced, I learned to embrace the unknown, trusting that I had the strength to rise above it.

She Leads

She leads is a declaration of empowerment. Leadership is not confined to a title or position; it is about influence, courage, and authenticity. As women, we possess an innate ability to lead—not only in our careers and communities but also in our own lives.

In my journey, I discovered that leading starts from within. It begins with self-acceptance and a commitment to our values. Leadership is about owning our story, embracing our truth, and using our experiences to inspire others. "What lies behind us and what lies before us are tiny matters compared to what lies within us," said Ralph Waldo Emerson, and this resonates deeply with me.

When I received my diagnosis, I knew that I had a choice. I could succumb to fear or I could lead myself through this tumultuous journey with grace and courage. I chose to lead. I became my own advocate, seeking knowledge about my condition, exploring treatment options, and connecting with others who had faced similar challenges. By sharing my story, I found strength not only for myself but also for those around me. I became a beacon of hope, showing others that they too could rise and lead in their own lives.

Leading also means empowering those around us. It is about lifting others as we climb, sharing our resources, knowledge, and experiences. Each time I share my journey, I am reminded of the countless women who have reached out to me for support. "We are stronger together," I tell them, encouraging them to embrace their own leadership potential. In lifting others, we create a ripple effect of empowerment that reverberates far beyond our immediate circles.

She Lives

Finally, she lives is an invitation to embrace life fully, even in the face of uncertainty. To live is to savor each moment, to find joy in the simplest of things, and to cultivate gratitude for the experiences that shape us.

In my experience, cancer has taught me the importance of living in the present. The diagnosis stripped away the trivial concerns that once consumed my thoughts. I learned to appreciate the beauty of each sunrise, the laughter of my children, and the warmth of a hug from a loved one. Life became an exquisite tapestry of moments, and I was determined to embrace every thread.

Living is also about taking risks and stepping outside our comfort zones. It is about pursuing our passions with fervor and not letting fear dictate our choices. I remember standing on the precipice of fear as I considered sharing my story publicly. "What if people judge me? What if they don't understand?" I thought. But then I realized that the only way to truly live was to embrace vulnerability. When I shared my journey, I found connection and support in the most unexpected places. I discovered that by living authentically, I was inviting others to do the same.

In those quiet moments of reflection, I would often find myself praying. Prayer became my lifeline, a source of comfort and strength. It allowed me to surrender my fears and uncertainties, opening my heart to the possibilities of what lay ahead. One of my favorite prayers became a mantra in my life: "Lord, grant me the serenity to accept the things I cannot change, courage to change the things I can, and wisdom to know the difference." This prayer encapsulated the essence of my journey— embracing the unknown while finding the strength to move forward.

A Warrior Spirit

To rise, lead, and live is to embody the spirit of a warrior. A warrior is not defined by their battles but by their resilience, tenacity, and unwavering spirit. We are all warriors, forged in the fires of our experiences, capable of overcoming even the most daunting challenges.

The warrior spirit teaches us to embrace our journey, however messy it may be. It reminds us that we are not alone; there are countless women who have walked similar paths, overcoming obstacles and defying the odds. Each story is a testament to our strength and a reminder that we can rise together.

As I reflect on my own journey, I am filled with gratitude for the lessons I have learned. I have discovered that vulnerability is not a weakness; it is a strength. I have learned that my story has the power to inspire others and create a ripple effect of hope. I have come to understand that by rising, leading, and living, I am not just surviving; I am thriving.

In conclusion, she rises. She leads. She lives—these words encapsulate the essence of my journey. They are a call to action, a reminder that we all possess the power to rise above our challenges, to lead with authenticity, and to live fully. As we navigate the complexities of life, let us embrace our warrior spirit and support one another in this beautiful journey. Together, we can rise, lead, and live in a world that needs our light more than ever.

Let us remember that in every moment of darkness, there is always a spark of hope waiting to be ignited. With every rise, we empower ourselves and those around us. With every lead, we create pathways for others to follow. And with every lived moment, we celebrate the beauty of life, even in the midst of uncertainty.

As I emerged from the shower that day, the steam still lingering in the air, I knew I was ready to embrace the journey ahead. I was determined to rise, to lead, and to live—fully and unapologetically. And as I stepped into the world, I carried those words with me, a reminder that I am a warrior, and I will always rise.

Paula Collins

Serene Wellness with Paula
Life Coach

https://www.facebook.com/groups/serenewellnesshealing/
https://www.instagram.com/serene.wellness.with.paula/
https://serenewellnesswithpaula.com/

Paula Collins is a Magdalene Priestess, Sound Healer, and Spirituality Mentor dedicated to empowering women to reclaim their sacred power and joy. With a unique blend of energy healing, sound therapy, and spiritual guidance, she helps women release conditioned beliefs and outdated values that limit their true potential. Through transformative practices rooted in ancient wisdom, she guides her clients to break free from generational patterns and rediscover their authentic selves. Her compassionate, holistic approach creates a safe space for deep healing, self-love, and spiritual awakening.

From Silence to Sovereignty: Reclaiming My Voice and Embracing My Authentic Self

By Paula Collins

I love my life. I love to wake up each morning to see what the day holds. I get giddy when I think about all that I can accomplish in my personal and professional life.

I am so content and fulfilled in my personal life. I have a partner who sees me for who I truly am and has no desires to change me. He accepts me fully and encourages me. He loves me unconditionally, is sweetly compassionate, and so forgiving. He has held me through the hard messy years of our lives, and now rejoices that I am whole.

It fills me with so much joy to know I have a beautiful circle of friends who are soul-aligned in beliefs and values. Just knowing the deep conversation and safe space to be vulnerable is so calming and peaceful.

I love my career as a Magdalene Sound Priestess. I have found my true calling and love to offer service and healing through private energy work, group sound baths, and Sabbat celebrations. It excites me when my clients see and feel the healing they have always wanted and cannot wait to see what shift will take place next.

But this has not always been the case. My path has not always been smooth and free of obstacles. I have overcome so much emotional trauma from the bullying I faced in junior high that caused social anxiety and people-pleasing tendencies.

For most of my childhood, I lived a pretty wonderful carefree life. I came from a loving home and had a few close friends to spend time with. I loved going to school, learning new things, and exploring my world.

But that all changed in junior high. Three girls made it their mission to torture me each day at recess. They would corner me and say the most horrible things to me. They would threaten me to the point that I would find ways to not enjoy recess anymore. I would ask if I could help any way in the classroom, if I could work in the lunch room, or even help out in the school office.

On the bus ride home from school, I would sit in the front seat alone so no one could hurt me. My only safe haven was home. We had only one phone and my parents were in charge of that. We did not have internet back in the 70s, so I had a place where I could just take a breath and not have to constantly look over my shoulder.

I never told anyone because that was part of the threats; of what they would do to me if I said anything to anyone. And I believed every word.

The defamation of character I received during that time would cause me to never speak my truth for fear of being belittled or cast away. So, I kept all my thoughts to myself unless they mirrored common thoughts.

I felt so isolated because whenever I wanted to make a new friend, I could hear the ugly words of my tormentors in my head telling me I was unwanted and unloveable. Whenever I wanted to try something new, I would hear the words in my head that I was stupid and worthless. Whenever I would try on clothing or hope that a cute boy would ask me out to the dance, I would hear those words telling me how ugly and pitiful I was and would always be. Whenever I would look in the mirror, I would see myself as my bullies painted me.

I hated going places where I didn't know anyone or only a few people. My anxiety would rise and I would freeze. I would find a spot where I did not have to interact with anyone, longing to be included. Even if I knew someone, if they were speaking to others, I would not interrupt or join in for fear of not being accepted or cast out. Social anxiety really sucks.

If anyone asked anything of me, I would jump at the prospect of helping. I would go out of my way, even canceling plans, just to help someone. I craved validation from others when I did something well. If you needed it, I was your girl. The "Yes" girl. The habitual people pleaser. It did not matter if I had other plans, I would cancel them just to feel included in some way. In many ways, it also made me a boundaryless doormat, which caused resentment and anger, but it didn't matter. I kept my feelings and opinions to myself.

Trying to constantly follow all the rules and be perfect became my coping mechanism. It was exhausting, but I was driven so strongly to do it to make up for all the shortcomings I believed I had because of someone else's definition of who I was. I had no real identity. I changed to fit the profile of who I was with or where I found myself. I learned the rules of their games and lives and created a persona that would be acceptable. It is a really shitty way to live and is so confusing. But it was my life.

I lived most of my adult life this way. I believed that in order to be loved I needed to accept others perceptions about what was true and real. I was so afraid that if someone really knew the true me, I would be alone. The fear that permeated everything I did and said.

I feared confrontation, so if someone's idea was different than mine, I kept my opinion to myself. I did anything I could to not cause an argument or disagreement of any kind. I just wasn't equipt at the time to have those discussions. Even when it came to choosing furniture or bed linens, I would defer to my husband. For so many years, he thought we had the exact same taste in everything. If someone told me my thoughts and opinions were not quite right, I would ask for their thoughts and then quickly adopt those. All I wanted was to belong.

Low self-esteem and low self-worth are so heavy to live with. Yet, even when I wanted to change, I could still hear the words and see the faces of my tormentors. It was constantly the echo in my ears and in my thoughts. I would wonder to myself when I was alone what people would say and think if they knew the real me. How would they act? I wondered what my life would look like if I spoke the words of my heart, if I chose the kind of life I wanted, if I acted in ways that made me happy, would I still have someone left to love me. I was constantly at war with myself, so I continued to play the role I had crafted over most of my life.

Have you ever heard about how a life-altering event can change everything? I always wondered about that when I would hear or read the stories. I tried to imagine how some event in a person's life could change their perspective and trajectory. It was hard to grasp until it happened to me.

In November of 2019, I was in a horrible car accident. I had no idea that trying to make a left-hand turn into a parking lot would cause an accident that would result in an injury that would change my life forever. But, it did.

The side impact I received caused injuries to me on so many levels. The biggest one would be my traumatic brain injury (TBI) which resulted in deficits I had to learn to live with. It affected my vision, hearing, constant tinnitus, and memory issues. So much so that I had to retire from a fulfilling teaching career because of it. The injury also affected my personal life and took away my ability to read for long periods of time, going out to concerts, movies, dancing, or being in loud restaurants.

At 50 years old, I had no idea what I would do with the rest of my life. I had to learn to navigate my new normal. It seemed like each day I found another limitation, and it caused a deep depression to settle in. I had lost so much and felt guilty about how these limitations affected my husband's life as well. Instead of enjoying all the things we used to do together, he had to find friends to do all those things with while I sat at home. In the beginning, it was hard. He felt guilty as well.

One day, while wallowing in self-pity and depression, a friend made a comment that would begin my change in perception. She said: "What if the accident didn't actually injure your brain, what if it healed it?" At first, I thought she was nuts, but that phrase continued to play out in my head. I started to ponder what it could really mean.

I think what helped me to hear it differently is that I was beginning a different path in my life at the same time. In trying to learn my new normal, I also started to listen to podcasts and watch documentaries about all sorts of subjects that piqued my interest. I was starting to think about my life differently because I had to, and this was the catalyst I needed to really begin anew.

I really started to delve into energy healing modalities and even found local practitioners who could help. Reiki was my number one go-to, and as I noticed the difference it could make in my life, I decided to learn it and offer it only to friends and family. I also found an intuitive life coach who used meridian tapping and found some success in releasing some of my trauma. Little by little, I started to see a shift taking place in my life. It was slow, but anything was better than what I was feeling.

I started to learn about shifting my mindset as well, so any time those negative thoughts crept in, I would try to rewrite them in positive ways so they would not cause me to spiral. Instead of having bad months, I started to only have a few bad days. I was amazed at how well this energy healing worked.

Some coping mechanisms were harder to break than others, but I kept at it. People pleasing was the hardest. I felt trapped by this one for a long time, but as I began to learn to create small boundaries in my personal life, I realized that these boundaries teach others how to treat me, what I would allow or accept in my life, and how I could finally begin to feel free. That was the best part. Did I lose some people along the way? Of course, I did. But you know what happened? I found out that I was acceptable, I was intelligent, I was creative, and I was loveable. I found out that I could speak my truth and people would not leave me. I found out that I could share my thoughts and opinions and people would listen and still love me. Do you know what a gift that can be?

I began to trust the most important person in my life: ME. I began to trust that she could make decisions and create a life that was fulfilling and filled with joy. I began to trust that as I introduced her to the world, the people who were meant to be a part of her life would show up. And you know what happened? I met some wonderful people who share the same values and we have the best conversations and so much fun together. One of the biggest surprises was how this all affected my husband. He has more joy in his life because he is not trying to fix me and be my savior. He loves discovering who I am at the core. He accepts me completely (not that he didn't love and accept me before).

The more I opened myself to healing my past, the more I discovered about myself. I realized I had gifts and talents I could share with others. I found that to be a true blessing. I realized I could use the energy healing modalities I already knew and combine them with intuitive gifts I was developing. I put my love of music to work in a new and exciting way through sound healing. I found out that when I offered these modalities to others, they actually would accept and trust me to help them. My life's purpose was unfolding right before my eyes, and I still get teary-eyed and goosebumps when I think about it.

One day, as I was listening to a webinar about Mary Magdalene, I had another revelation. I was called to work with her in a new and exciting way. I contacted the woman who held the webinar and set up a time to talk to her. During our conversation, I realized that the deep spirituality I was developing was opening me to the possibility of becoming a Priestess. She agreed, and a new journey began. I reveled in the course work and learned to call back my power to me. The power I had unknowingly given away to other people through my old coping mechanisms was returning to me and empowering me in body, mind, and spirit. I was on fire and realized that this was the authentic me I had been searching for. This was the me I was created to be. This was the me I wanted to share with world.

I am now a Magdalene Sound Priestess who leads ceremonies, offers courses that are life-changing for my clients, facilitates retreats that allow for deep and unbounded change, and knows and speaks the truth.

I get to know my clients on such a deep level, that I can develop one-on-one sessions and group sessions that allow them to call back their power and live in their own authenticity. It is humbling to be trusted to guide women, but I understand where they are because I was there. I create something so special and nurturing for them that they feel the confidence and self-love they have longed for. I lead by example and through experience.

So the question becomes: How do you want to live and experience your life? Do you want to continue down a road that keeps you right where you are? Sure, that is easy, even if it is difficult and lacks joy, because at least you know what to expect each day. Right? You may even think to yourself, I am too old to change, or maybe I am not supposed to experience ease and joy. You may even think: It has always been this way. At least I know it, so I know what to expect and how to protect myself. But is that any way to truly live? Always waiting for the next bad thing to happen or always ready for the fight?

Imagine for a moment if it could be different. Imagine if you could wake up each day excited for what unfolds. Imagine if you could still experience joy even in the tough times. Imagine if you could change your mindset and adopt a new way of being.

Imagine if you could get in touch with your soul deep inside of you. Imagine if you could experience the joy of seeing your dreams and desires come true. Imagine if you actually could remember the authentic you that you were meant to be and live that authentic life. How would that change your perception or your worldview?

Take a moment to stop and reflect on your life. Maybe even get a journal and write about it. Where in your life have you been playing it small? When have you kept your thoughts to yourself for fear of persecution or being turned away? When have you changed who you are just to fit in?

Now, look at those answers. Those are the times and places where you have given your power away to someone else. Isn't it time to call that back to you?

Feel free to reach out to me to learn more about how you can reclaim your sacred power and start living the life you were meant for.

Beth Ann Kaib

Owner of Nomadic Cowgirl

https://www.linkedin.com/in/bethannkaib/
https://www.facebook.com/nomadiccowgirl/
https://www.instagram.com/allthingsbeth.nomadiccowgirl/
https://www.allthingsbeth.com/

My name is Beth Ann, and I am an international best-selling author, serial entrepreneur, and humanitarian with a lifelong dedication to serving others. Throughout my career, I've worked in customer service, non-profits, and the medical field, focusing on helping special needs children and working with therapeutic programs involving horses. My primary business is Nomadic Cowgirl, where I operate as a Visionary Framework Strategist, Web Designer, and Virtual Assistant, specializing in supporting small businesses. My goal is to help entrepreneurs build or rebuild a solid framework that enhances their business success. I offer services that range from guiding new businesses through their launch to creating functional, appealing websites and providing administrative assistance. My work is all about empowering small business owners to achieve their visions, streamline their operations, and grow sustainably. Through Nomadic Cowgirl, I'm committed to making a lasting impact on the businesses and lives of those I work with.

The Road to Rebuilding

By Beth Ann Kaib

As a little girl, I was surrounded by them. My mom, grandmas, aunts, the random woman at the grocery store, and Snow White. Women taking care of men. The world showed me that the purpose of a woman is to take care of a man. So, I did. The world didn't prepare me for what happened next.

We were like lots of other modern-day couples. I bought my first house, and we moved in together before we were engaged, though, the engagement quickly followed, as did planning the wedding. That's when there was a shift in the air. He began to have sleepless nights, became agitated easily, and questioned if I really loved him. Cold feet... right?

After so many long, intense conversations, we took the plunge a few months later. Surrounded by the ones we loved, we said, "I do." Then, we were off for our romantic getaway. This honeymoon phase of our marriage was full of fighting and lacked intimacy. I couldn't wrap my head around what was happening. Things surely had to change once we got back to our comfortable surroundings.

Except, they didn't. That's when things escalated. Random items started appearing around the house and in the backyard. Tools, bikes, a motorcycle, guns, and random décor started coming home with him regularly. I was accused of cheating, called a slut, lazy, and the scum on the bottom of his shoe. I was expected to have home-cooked meals made and ready for him when HE was ready for dinner, even if that was nine o'clock at night. I quickly spiraled into depression and wondered if this was what marriage was meant to be.

Another day, another load of laundry. What did I find in this load of laundry? A small ziplock baggie of methamphetamine. The lightbulbs started going off in my head. Everything was adding up. I started researching all the signs and symptoms of meth use online. My fairly innocent country girl's mind was blown.

As I sat there with a bag of meth in one hand and a cell phone in the other, I contemplate all the choices I could think of. Do I call the cops and send him to prison? Do I call my husband? His best friend? What if it wasn't his? But then why was it in his load of work clothes? Do I admit failure and leave him? Doesn't he love me enough to quit? This is my husband; do I continue to take care of him?

I cried. I was an ugly, hot, uncontrollable mess. I was isolated. No one knew what was truly happening behind closed doors. I didn't allow anyone to know. I went down a deep, dark hole of wondering what was wrong with me. What was I doing wrong in my wifely duties? Well, he had no problem identifying and telling me what I was doing wrong on a daily basis. The name-calling, insults, expectations, and paranoia became even worse. I was not allowed to be around his brother-in-law or his father because he thought we were flirting. I wasn't allowed to have a one-on-one conversation with any of his female family members on the phone or in person at family functions unless he was present. I wasn't allowed to spend money without his approval and had to print out weekly bank statements for him to review. I wasn't allowed to say no in the bedroom. That's when the physical aggression started too. He started throwing things, kicking things, and leaving holes in the wall. Nothing was ever his fault. I always caused him to do it.

Still, I stayed to take care of my husband. That was my job. Clean up the constant mess he left behind. Clean and reorganize his work truck when he came crashing down from his drug use. Deliver food to his job site because he had already eaten the lunch I packed him and was still hungry. Take an Uber to meet him in the middle of the night, on the side of the road forty miles away, so I could drive the work truck home because he couldn't stay awake. Even fill a container at his boss's request so he could pass a drug test. All while working a full-time job and raising my special needs daughter.

Somehow, the years went by, three of them, with many failed attempts to help him get clean. I believed everything he told me I was. I failed at life and as a wife. I didn't recognize my reflection in the mirror anymore. I didn't realize how bad it was until my daughter was forced to show me.

While all of this was happening, I was also preparing for my daughter to have brain surgery. After a series of psychological, physical, speech, and occupational therapy evaluations, the day finally arrived. My daughter and I sat with the neurologist in the very last doctor's office appointment a couple of weeks before brain surgery. That's when the doctor asked me to leave the room. Little did I know that was the start of the moment that changed my life.

The rest of that appointment was a blur. The next thing I remember was pushing my daughter's wheelchair through the parking lot out to the car and loading her up. We sat there in silence for what felt like an eternity. She was fidgeting with the strings on her hoodie, her eyes staring at the floor, and had a tear rolling down her cheek. That's when she said it. She was afraid to go home. She was scared for my safety. Not hers but mine.

With one shocking phone call to my parents, I was on the move. I packed the entire contents of her room, a bag for myself, grabbed my dog and walked out of the first house I owned before he got home from work. My parents provided a room in their house for my daughter and me to stay in. I was so grateful to have a place where my daughter could feel safe.

I had to adjust to living back home with my parents while my daughter was about to go through a series of four brain surgeries. This was on top of a divorce with a soon-to-be ex-husband that wouldn't leave me alone. Not a day went by without a reminder from him. There were endless emails, letters, gifts on my truck, drive-bys and who knows how many texts and phone calls after I blocked his number. I still didn't feel safe. His voice still echoed in my head daily. You are so lazy. You don't make enough money. My dinner wasn't cooked right. The house isn't clean enough. You are no better than the scum on the bottom of my shoe. You are broken. I was full of shame, embarrassment, and hatred for myself.

Life continued to move forward even though I wasn't ready. As I watched my daughter, still asleep from anesthesia with her head wrapped in gauze in the recovery room after her first brain surgery, the reality of my life quickly set in. The cost of living, houses and life in general increased so much that I realized I would not be able to buy another house on my own any time soon. How could I help my daughter heal while I was so broken and stuck? As I looked at her, I saw the reflection of defeat in my daughter's eyes. I was determined to show her that no matter what, you can rebuild yourself even stronger. The only way to show her that was by example. But how?

After she was discharged and we were back at my parents' house, I went on a deep dive through Google, researching alternative living arrangements. That's when I learned about four ladies who were friends, all living in RVs, full-time traveling across the country. They were hosting an online event to learn all about the lifestyle. I was intrigued, so I attended. As I watched interviews, I was reminded of one summer when I was a kid, and my parents took me across the country in a fifth wheel. I wondered if this could be my answer.

I did what any semi-rational human being would do, and I bought a travel trailer. While my daughter was going through her remaining 3 brain surgeries, I completely renovated it to fit her unique needs. Everyone thought I was nuts. How was a single mom with a special needs child going to travel across the country in a travel trailer?

As soon as she was healed and we had the doctor's clearance, we left. My goal was to escape my ex-husband. Nothing else mattered. Little did I know that this trip was going to be a pivotal turning point in my life.

If you have ever spent time in RV life, you know that things break and go wrong constantly. Thanks to my father for raising me so independently, I was equipped to fix everything that physically broke on that trip. The empty space between my kid and me, the constant song of defeat running through my head—that was a different story. I had to figure that out and fast. I couldn't keep that broken mindset while keeping my daughter and me safe in unfamiliar areas throughout the country.

This adventure started a long path of healing and self-discovery. I knew I wasn't done in life. I began to realize I was meant for more and that I deserved to be happy. I also knew I had to heal myself first. I started changing the narrative in my head with baby steps. "You are lazy" turned into "Yeah, you are lazy compared to him, but you aren't relying on stimulants to get through life." "You don't make enough" turned into "You make enough money to be out here traveling across the country." "You are no better than the scum on the bottom of his shoe" became "I may be scum, but I am no longer on the bottom of his shoe." It wasn't pretty, but it was a start. The narrative in my head was changing.

The trials on the road quickly became triumphs. I could finally back up the trailer on the first attempt. I could hook up and unhook the trailer in a matter of minutes. The water pump blew in the truck. I had it handled. The campground was overbooked, the rest stop was full, and the tires overheated—I handled it all. I began to find my strength in the trials and tribulations. I started to take all the doubts, insecurities, and negative thoughts that cluttered my mind and repurpose them as fuel. Every piece of "crap" that once weighed me down became a stepping stone, each one driving me to push past my own limitations. My mission became clear: to rewrite the narrative in my head, to replace the voice of self-doubt with one of self-belief and resilience. As I posted our adventure on social media, that narrative changed too. People were complimenting my strength, envious of our adventure, and wanting to know how I was doing it. Most importantly, my daughter and I were talking and laughing together again.

As I sat on the side of the mountain and stared out into the sky, I realized everything was changing quickly. I began to enjoy the beauty that surrounded us. I heard the wind blowing through the pine trees and the birds singing. I saw the sun shining on the wildflowers dancing at my feet. It was no longer about escape, but about rebuilding myself.

As I continued on this journey, something powerful happened—I realized I was healing. I wasn't broken, as I had once believed. In truth, I was transforming. Beneath all the scars and struggles, there was a light within me that was starting to shine, brighter than ever. I wasn't just surviving anymore; I was glowing, radiating the strength and resilience I had cultivated through my trials. And with this glow, I embraced a new chapter, one where I began to understand my worth and the incredible power I held within.

Now that I was healing, it was time for me to figure out what I wanted for myself, and it was time to include my daughter. Somewhere in the middle of the country, I decided to start a business. I knew what I wanted to do with my business, but I didn't know what to name my business. We quickly got to work.

We had a full-length mirror on the outside of the bathroom door. Our mission was to write down all the words that described who I was on that mirror. It took several days, but by the time we were done, my reflection was completely covered. My objective was to name my business and include my daughter in the process. I never imagined that this task would help me see that I was far more than I had ever given myself credit for.

After dinner one night, it was time. We sat at the table and stared at the mirror. Which words didn't resonate or sound great? We began to erase words off the mirror, one word at a time. We were down to two words on the mirror. The word "Cowgirl" in red on the upper left corner of the mirror and "Nomad" in green on the lower right. My daughter proudly announced, "That's it! You are a Nomadic Cowgirl." With that, my business was born, and a spark was reignited in my daughter's eyes.

Although we had to return to my parents' house shortly after this due to COVID, our journey of growth didn't stop there. She enrolled in an accelerated college program and even began taking horseback riding lessons. Meanwhile, I focused on expanding my business and found a creative outlet through writing.

As I write this chapter, it's been five years since I returned from that trip. I have faced many trials and tribulations since then. Each time, I remember that we don't have to turn ourselves into broken figures. We have a choice. We can use those broken feelings as fuel and motivation to push us past our current limitations. We can transmute the crap that fills our heads into stepping stones in life.

If I didn't go through feeling broken, I would not have found my true, happy, whole, healed self that I am now. Without those trials, I would have never found my true strength. I would not have had the perseverance to become an entrepreneur or an international best-selling author. I wouldn't appreciate the true love that I now have for another. I wouldn't have learned that it's not about the circumstances in life, it's how we view the situation. I don't even recognize a broken person within me anymore.

So, I ask you, what self-deprecating thoughts are running through your head? What false things have you been told that you are still believing? What words do you need to change the narrative on? How can you turn the crap that fills your head into fuel and motivation? What current limitations have you set on yourself that you can break free from?

I share my story with you for the sole purpose of inspiring you to never give up!

Cindy Hartzell

Heart Soul Confidence-Based Horsemanship®
Horsemanship Mentor & Transformational Coach

https://www.facebook.com/heartsoulconfidencebasedhorsemanship
https://www.instagram.com/confidencebasedhorsemanship/
https://heartsoulhorsemanship.com

Cindy Hartzell is a passionate horsemanship motivational coach and the founder of Heart Soul Connections, a transformative program designed to help women reconnect with their inner selves through the healing power of horses. With over forty years of experience working with horses, Cindy has dedicated her life to nurturing the bond between women and these magnificent creatures. Her journey began with her own battles for self-worth and inner peace, finding solace in the silent understanding of horses. Through personal trials, including traumatic injuries and the loss of her cherished horse, RC, Cindy discovered the profound resilience that lies within. She now guides others in overcoming obstacles, embracing vulnerability, and thriving against all odds. Her work is a testament to the power of love, connection, and the human spirit's ability to rise, lead, and live fully. Through her story, Cindy inspires others to find their path to healing and self-discovery.

Rising from the Ashes

By Cindy Hartzell

Introduction: The Catalyst for Change

The relationship between a horse and a human is unlike any other. It is a silent bond, a dance of trust, love, and mutual respect. My journey of "She Rises" began with RC, my palomino. RC came to me as a wild yearling from a PMU (Pregnant Mare Urine) horse rescue group in North Dakota. Like mine, his early life was a testament to survival against all odds.

The PMU industry, where RC came from, involves confining pregnant mares to collect their urine, which contains hormones used to produce estrogen supplements, such as Premarin, for women in menopause. This practice has drawn criticism for its harsh treatment of the mares, who are kept in narrow stalls, often referred to as "stocks," restricting their movement. They endure long periods tethered with urinary catheters and collection bags to extract their urine for hormone production. Sadly, this industry also produces a large number of foals as unwanted byproducts. For many years, these foals were shipped off to auctions and often faced slaughter. However, thanks to the compassion of rescue groups, some foals, like RC, were given a chance at life through adoption.

RC's story, and that of many others, sheds light on the complexities and ethical concerns of the PMU industry, including not only the treatment of mares and foals but also the health risks associated with PMU-derived hormone supplements. Studies have linked products like Premarin to an increased risk of breast cancer and other health issues, underscoring the importance of seeking more humane and healthier alternatives.

For eleven years, RC and I forged a connection that went beyond the physical. We danced together, explored the wilderness, and studied the fine art of horsemanship, synchronizing our hearts and souls.

In May of 2019, everything changed. What was supposed to be a regular training session with RC and a young mustang ended in a freak accident. In the process of tying RC to the trailer, he pulled back unexpectedly. My fingers were caught and sucked up into the cleat, resulting in the amputation of one finger and the loss of the tip of another. It was a shocking, traumatic event that marked the beginning of a new chapter in my life—a chapter of fear, healing, and profound self-discovery.

The Pain of Disconnect: Finding the Source

The physical pain of losing my fingers was intense, but the emotional aftermath was far more excruciating. Almost immediately, I sensed a change in the connection between RC and myself. This wasn't just about the accident. It felt deeper, more significant. The bond we had nurtured over a decade seemed to fray, leaving an emptiness that I couldn't ignore. For weeks, I avoided him, opting instead to spend time with the other horses in our herd. I rationalized my absence as part of the healing process, but the truth was harder to admit: I didn't trust RC anymore, and more poignantly, I didn't trust myself.

Watching RC from a distance, I noticed that he, too, had changed. His once vibrant, confident demeanor had turned quiet and withdrawn. It was clear—he was feeling the disconnect just as much as I was. We were both lost, trying to navigate the uncharted waters of our new reality.

Confronting Fear: The Emotional Abyss

I had faced trauma before—broken bones, concussions, a traumatic brain injury that had left me unconscious for fifteen minutes in 2017. But this was different. The disconnection I felt with RC wasn't about physical pain; it was about trust. The incident made me realize that beneath the surface of our relationship lay a foundation that had been shaken. It wasn't just about what RC had done; it was about what the accident symbolized. My source of joy, comfort, and peace had become a source of fear. I was terrified of getting hurt again, not just physically, but emotionally.

Joseph Campbell's words echoed in my mind: "It is by going down into the abyss that we recover the treasures of life. Where you stumble, there lies your treasure." I had to confront the abyss within my soul, face the fears that held me captive, and find the treasures buried in my pain. It wasn't about blaming RC or even myself. It was about understanding that this accident was a catalyst—a chance to go deeper, to uncover parts of myself I had buried long ago.

The Journey to Reconnection: Trusting the Process

The journey of reconnection began slowly. I started spending undemanding time with RC, simply being in his presence without any expectations. Our interactions were tentative, filled with the awkwardness of two beings who had once been close but now felt like strangers. I had to quiet my mind, calm the storm of emotions raging within me, and allow myself to feel everything. The tension in my chest, the butterflies in my stomach, the tightness in my throat—all these sensations were messages from my body, urging me to stay, to face the discomfort, and not run away.

Healing is a process, one that requires patience, compassion, and honesty. I had to be honest with myself about the fear I felt, the distrust that lingered, and the uncertainty of our future together. I couldn't fake it. Horses, like RC, are intuitive beings. They sense our energy, feel our emotions, and reflect back what we project. Pretending to be okay when I wasn't would only create more distance. I had to show up authentically, embrace the vulnerability, and allow myself to heal alongside RC.

The Mirror of the Soul: Horses as Teachers

Horses are mirrors, reflecting our deepest emotions and fears. They teach us to be present, to listen to our instincts, and to be true to ourselves. As I navigated my healing journey, RC became my teacher. He showed me the importance of authenticity, of being present in the moment and not hiding behind a mask of false confidence. Through our time together, I realized that the only way to overcome the trauma was to confront it head-on, lean into the discomfort, and embrace the lessons it had to offer.

This journey wasn't just about rebuilding my relationship with RC; it was about rebuilding my relationship with myself. Horses, with their gentle yet powerful presence, have a unique ability to bring us face-to-face with our true selves. They don't judge, but they don't lie either. They reflect back our energy, showing us the parts of ourselves we may try to hide. RC showed me the fears I had buried, the insecurities I had tried to ignore, and the strength I possessed to rise above them.

Unveiling the Inner Child: A Journey Through Shadows

As I delved deeper into my healing, memories from my past resurfaced. I remembered the child I once was, a little girl raised to be seen and not heard, disciplined for speaking out, and finding solace in the company of horses. My early years were filled with confusion and a sense of not belonging. Horses were my refuge, my escape from the chaos of a world that didn't understand me. They provided a sense of freedom, a way to connect with my true self when everything else felt wrong.

The trauma I experienced with RC was more than just a freak accident; it was a mirror reflecting my unresolved past. I realized that the fear I felt wasn't just about losing fingers; it was about losing a part of myself. The little girl who found solace in horses was still inside me, still seeking the love, acceptance, and freedom she had longed for as a child. I had spent years trying to protect her, hiding her away to keep her safe, but now it was time to set her free.

Burning Down the Prison: Reclaiming Freedom

Joseph Campbell said, "Opportunities to find deeper powers within ourselves come when life seems most challenging." The accident with RC was my opportunity to discover the deeper powers within me, to confront the shadows that had kept me captive for so long. It was time to burn down the prison of fear, guilt, and shame that had defined my life. It was time to reclaim my freedom.

In a symbolic act of release, I imagined the prison walls I had built around my heart burning down to the ground. I saw myself standing amidst the ashes, holding the hand of my inner child, feeling the weight of the past lifting from my shoulders. It was a moment of liberation, a declaration that I was no longer bound by the chains of my past. I had the power to create a new reality, one where I could live authentically, without fear, without shame.

Embracing Vulnerability: The Path to Authenticity

Rebuilding my relationship with RC meant embracing vulnerability. It meant showing up in my rawest, most authentic form and allowing myself to be seen. Vulnerability is often seen as a weakness, but it is one of our greatest strengths. It takes courage to be vulnerable and to admit that we are scared, hurt, and unsure. But in that vulnerability lies the power to connect, to heal, and to rise.

As I allowed myself to be vulnerable with RC, our bond began to strengthen. The emptiness I had felt started to fade, replaced by a sense of connection that was deeper than before. It wasn't about returning to what we had; it was about creating something new. Our relationship had evolved, and so had I. I was no longer the same person I was before the accident. I had grown, and with that growth came a new understanding of what it meant to truly connect—with myself and with RC.

The Power of Presence: Living in the Moment

One of the greatest lessons horses teach us is the power of presence. They live in the moment, not dwelling on the past or worrying about the future. They remind us to be here, now, to experience life as it unfolds. In the aftermath of the accident, I had been consumed by thoughts of what could have been, how I could have prevented it, and what it meant for the future. But RC showed me that the only moment that truly matters is the present one.

Being present means letting go of the need to control and allowing ourselves to be guided by the flow of life. It means trusting that we are exactly where we need to be, even if it doesn't make sense at the time. It means embracing the uncertainty and finding peace in the midst of chaos. Through RC, I learned to quiet my mind, to breathe, and to be present with what was. I learned that healing isn't a destination; it's a journey, one that unfolds moment by moment.

Rising Strong: The Journey of "She Rises"

The journey of "She Rises" is about more than overcoming obstacles; it's about thriving against all odds. It's about finding the strength within to face the darkest parts of ourselves and emerge stronger. It's about embracing the challenges that life throws our way and using them as opportunities for growth. Learning to recognize that our greatest struggles are often the catalysts for our greatest transformations.

RC and I have come a long way since that fateful day in May. Our bond is not the same as it was before—it's deeper, more authentic, and more resilient. We have both risen from the ashes, learning to trust again, to love again, and to live again. The journey hasn't been easy, but it has been worth it. Through the pain, the fear, and the uncertainty, I have discovered a strength within myself that I never knew existed. I have found my way back to my true self, the person I was always meant to be.

Conclusion: Living Authentically, Leading Fearlessly

The journey of "She Rises" is one of self-discovery, healing, and empowerment. It's about embracing who we are, flaws and all, and living our truth. It's about leading fearlessly, not because we are unafraid, but because we choose to rise above our fears. It's about finding the courage to live authentically, to be vulnerable, and to connect with others on a deeper level.

As a horsemanship motivational coach, I help others navigate their own journeys of healing and self-discovery. I help them find their way back to their true selves, to reclaim their power, and to live their lives with purpose and passion. Through my work with RC and the other horses, I have learned that the path to healing is not a straight line; it's a winding road filled with twists, turns, and unexpected detours. But it is a road worth traveling, for it leads to the treasures of life.

In the end, the journey of "She Rises" is about living fully, loving deeply, and leading with an open heart. It's about recognizing that the obstacles we face are not there to break us but to build us. It's about finding the strength to rise, the courage to lead, and the grace to live. For it is in rising that we discover who we truly are, in leading that we find our purpose, and in living that we fulfill our destiny.

> **"A hero is someone who has given his or her life to something bigger than oneself."**
> —Joseph Campbell

I am that hero, and so are you. Together, we rise.

Kim Diamond

Founder and CEO of PhoneSpuds

https://www.linkedin.com/in/kim-diamond-phonespuds/
https://www.facebook.com/kim.bloomdiamond/
https://www.instagram.com/liquidkim
https://www.phonespuds.com/

Kim Diamond is an expert on creative coping and resilience, who's been seen on Season 14 of Wes Bergmann's entrepreneur reality TV show, The Blox. She started her career in media sales, and began working on her potato-themed pillow phone stand product, PhoneSpuds, during her long covid and concussion recovery in 2021.

Kim is an abuse and sexual assault survivor. In March 2020, she fell ill with covid and experienced lingering symptoms for 3 years. Kim's recovery was compounded by a head injury in January 2021, which left her using a walker. Despite this, Kim launched her product, PhoneSpuds, in 2023. She is also a former English teacher.

Today, when she's not singing, writing poetry, or walking her dog, you'll find her encouraging other entrepreneurs and working on new prototypes.

To learn more about Kim and how she can help you personally or professionally, visit www.phonespuds.com.

After 5, It's All Rainbows & Ponies

By Kim Diamond

What is it that gives us the strength to keep moving forward during life's most difficult seasons? How can we remain true to ourselves and not become jaded after taking a mental, physical, or emotional blow? I've heard a variety of responses to this question throughout my life, mostly during times when I was the one asking it. The answers are most commonly religion, meditation, therapy, acceptance, music, fitness, writing, and the list goes on... The strategies that have helped me resurrect after pain and loss have more to do with mindset than what coping mechanism you're trying.

I don't want to write a chapter about all the difficult things I've faced, because that's not the focus. Those tough life experiences are important for context, but I want to focus on the moving forward. So, in the interest of not dramatizing anything or triggering anyone, I'm structuring my chapter as such:

a. My Little Life Timeline
b. Strategies for Moving Forward
c. Poetry

I am a gentle person by nature with strong apologetic social programming. That said, the work I've done to move forward in life is important. Helping others empowers me and gives me the strength to keep going when hard memories resurface.

My Little Life Timeline

Childhood	neglect / hunger
	emotional & physical abuse
	sex abuse
	bullying
High School	discovered theatre
	top AP English score in Iowa
College	leadership scholarship from Northern Michigan University (NMU)
	performed last minute as Adelaide in *Guys & Dolls* *defining moment*
	graduated with a double major in Performance Theatre and English
	received Secondary Education Teaching Certification
My 20s	taught high school English & directed school plays / musicals
	married
	domestic violence (3 years)
	divorce
	moved to Maryland / DC area
	worked in advertising sales for military trade magazines
	traveled extensively for work
	drugged & sexually assaulted while attending a work event
	moved to Upstate NY

	diagnosed with PTSD
	peeping Tom, leading to stalking & home invasion
	moved back to Maryland / DC area
My 30's	met & fell in love with my partner, Chris Diamond
	diagnosed with cPTSD
	worked for historic architecture trade magazines & events
	worked part-time as a lounge singer
	Chris's breakdown, leading to relocation to Iowa
	lead singer in a local radio station rock band (7 years)
	daughter Charlotte born
	worked remotely for historic architecture magazines
	miscarriage #1
	stalking, leading to being drugged & sexually assaulted
	miscarriage #2
	Chris diagnosed with Acute Myeloid Leukemia (AML) / I was his caregiver
My 40's	breakdown / return to therapy for cPTSD
	Chris and I separated
	acute COVID infection leading to long COVID illness
	Our child's sexual abuse & court proceedings
	Chris and I reconcile
	severe concussion from an at-home accident, which left me using a walker

	heart impacts from COVID-19 discovered
	extensive physical & occupational therapy
	denied adoption due to my illness and injury
	began substitute teaching
	had the idea for my pillow phone stand product, PhoneSpuds
	taught high school English for 1 year
	launched PhoneSpuds
	unable to continue teaching due to post-concussion syndrome
	competed on The Blox reality TV show, Season 14
on-going	disability & entrepreneur journey

Not Giving Up

It was 2005. I lay curled up in a bathrobe on the family room floor of the house I was renting in Rome, NY. I had only lived there a couple of months, because I had been living in the neighboring village, Barneveld, with my boyfriend, Brian. He was one of my best friends from college. We had reconnected when I was living in Maryland, and he was traveling to the DC area on business. He worked for a defense contractor.

I ended the relationship and moved to Rome, NY, to start over, because Brian was still heavily into the drinking culture of our college years. I was newly divorced from my abusive ex, Aaron, and I jumped into things with Brian too quickly. One night when the nightmares became overwhelming, I took about 13 Xanax in order to fall asleep, and woke up in the mental health unit in a nearby Utica hospital. I was officially diagnosed with PTSD during that stay and knew that I had to end things with Brian. Our relationship was too chaotic, and it was clear to me that he was an alcoholic. I thought that being in my own space would help me feel safe and have control over my environment.

While that was true to a point, I really didn't feel safer. I was alone and scared and hurting. I worked remotely for a new homeland security magazine that recruited me from one of the conferences I attended when I worked for the military magazines. I'm a workaholic, so working remotely was no problem for me. I represented the magazine at trade shows throughout the country, and I grew my sales territory from zero to the top-performing territory in 5 months.

However, after the hospital stay, I was severely paralyzed mentally and emotionally. I was a puddle on the floor in front of the TV, unable to eat, unable to sleep, barely bathing, and hardly moving from my spot in the middle of the family room.

I was adamantly opposed to the thought of having PTSD. It felt like if I accepted it, I was giving my ex, and the man who had sexually assaulted me a few years prior during a work event in DC, power over me. I couldn't accept that. Still, I knew that I was unable to function, and I had never experienced that before. I began popping over-the-counter medicines, trying to numb myself. I went to the therapy that I had been assigned to after leaving the hospital. But really, it took a few weeks of hibernating before I could do anything.

We all have a breaking point, and it felt like I had inadvertently found mine. So, I lay on the floor with my cats, my phone, and a spread of papers around me. I watched episodes of La Femme Nikita (the one with Peta Wilson). I was angry at myself all the time. Never in my life had I had an issue with functioning like this. So, when I couldn't get in the shower or get myself to eat lunch, I gave myself zero grace. All the nasty things that I had been programmed to believe about myself, whether from childhood, my ex-husband, or general social programming, I flung at myself. I knew the doctors were right about PTSD, and I had admitted it to the therapist. But I didn't discuss any of the details of my assault or abuse with anyone; it felt like by giving voice to it, I was validating it, and I wouldn't do that.

Some time into my haze of dissociation and depression, I started writing 3 bullet points on a piece of paper every day. I remember talking to my parents, and telling my mom that I was going to try and do just 3 things. Every day, I focused on only the 3 things I wrote down. They were usually a variation of 1) eat something, 2) call someone, 3) shower, etc.... I almost never got the 3 things accomplished for the day, at least not for a while. In particular, showering is very hard for me when I'm triggered, even to this day.

I was lucky that I had the work situation that I did, during this time of emotional collapse. If I hadn't already met my quota in the weeks leading up to this, I wouldn't have had the financial freedom to be completely dysfunctional for weeks. I don't know if I would've pulled myself together sooner because I needed the money, or if I would've lingered in meltdown mode and moved home to my parents in Iowa. I'm pretty sure I would've pulled myself together sooner because the idea of moving home to Iowa was the antithesis of everything I wanted. I wanted to get back to the DC area, where I felt most at home. My overall plan was to live in Rome and save the money to move back. So, day by day, I tried to accomplish just 3 basic things. Eventually, the list became 4 things and 5 things, and by allowing myself time, I became more capable.

Gradually, I started fighting back to overcome the paralysis. I started making rules for myself to help move forward. One of them was to avoid watching crime dramas or other potentially triggering things on TV. I started referring to this rule as, "After 5, it's all rainbows & ponies." I had taken to watching Criminal Minds and realized that I needed to be done with it for a while (at least in the evening). I also started leaving my house each day to work out at the local YMCA. Because I was working from home, I realized that I had to find reasons to leave the house. I didn't have a wholly healthy attitude about this, in fact, much of my working out was more like self-punishment. I was tricking my body into doing healthy things in the name of punishment.

As I was coming out of the fog, and leaving the house more, I started to notice my patio chairs and a variety of other objects moved beneath my windows; it was cat litter buckets, chairs, planters, just a variety of things. Then, one night, I was getting out of the shower and saw him. A man was standing outside my bathroom window with his face pressed up against the glass watching me. He had a blue beanie on. I immediately pounded on the window with my fist and let out a scream. My windows had a covering on them, but it was like a cling that peeled on. Other windows were heavily covered with curtains, but apparently, the surface was less protective and shielding to the naked eye than it appeared on my side of the glass. Because Brian was hanging out with me that night, he went running out after the man. It was no use, the guy had a headstart, and there was no one in sight.

We called the police, and sure enough, the man had left fingerprints all over my downstairs windows. They took the prints and told me to call if I saw him again or if anything else seemed off. I spent a few nights back at Brian's until I felt brave enough to go back. I really believed the police could protect me, and I thought the fingerprints would lead to an arrest. I covered every window with extra heavy curtains, and I asked the landlord to add motion lights all over the property. I was terrified, but I also was ready to spit nails. I was so angry. Here I was, trying to recover from sexual assault and domestic violence, ending another relationship in a different town, and some pervert decided to peep at me.

Five months passed, and one night getting out of the tub, I heard a slam. I called the police, and they discovered the man had been entering my cellar (which opened to the backyard). On my side, it opened to my bathroom. When I asked the police about the fingerprints, I learned they had not even been processed yet. Terrified and disgusted, I stayed at Brian's, hired movers, and went home to Iowa to the safety of my parents. I felt hunted. I resolved to save money by working in Iowa and staying at home for my eventual return to Maryland, and that is exactly what I did.

I'm sharing this snapshot of my life for a few reasons. First, I want to show where I've risen from. Sadly, each of these experiences is also highly relatable to other women. The other point I want to share here is that rising out of abuse, assault, grief, depression, or anything really, is not pretty. It's messy. And in life, you may be able to move forward through life after adversity or trauma, but that doesn't mean you're not going to feel the pain and the fear. Some of my poems became songs, and I'm reminded of the lyrics to a song Sorry Girl, that I'm still working on. It goes, "I can take whatever hit. Don't tell me not to feel it." It's important to know, there's no way to skip the pain. You've got to move *through* it.

When you're digging yourself out of an emotional pit, you don't feel strong, at least, I didn't. You can't avoid the part where it hurts like Hell. I wish there were another way, but I've learned over and over again in my life that putting one foot in front of the other to move on is a battle, and it hurts. It sometimes leaves scars and other damage that you have to deal with. But, if you're not ending your own life and you're still trying to get up, you are rising. You're gonna feel it, and that's okay. That's normal. It's only when you stop trying that you become truly defeated. Even when I was lying in a nest of blankets on the family room floor, I had my notepad, and I wrote 3 things. I still tried. And I kept on trying until I was able to do it—and more.

I wish I could say this was the only time in my life that I had to claw my way out of the abyss, but it's not. However, the fact that I did it this time helped me to know down the road when I was struggling, that I could pull myself out of it. And as I got older, I became more skilled at rising. I started being more gentle with myself and with others. And the pain became less disheartening and more a reminder that I'm alive and that I have things to fight for. No battle feels good. It's always hard. Accepting that is an important step in moving on.

Breaking Point

I met my husband and partner, Chris Diamond, in 2008 in Washington, DC. I had taken the metro red line down to Dupont Circle to have a drink at a bar called, The Big Hunt. I was pregaming for a night out dancing, and one of my friends was meeting me there later, so we could bounce around the clubs together.

I was passing the time at the busy dive bar by putting songs into the jukebox, mostly Nick Cave & The Bad Seeds songs, and I especially enjoyed subjecting the crowd to the song, *From Her to Eternity*, which was particularly loud (and some may say obnoxious). I didn't see the man making his way through the crowd over to me, because I was finishing my song selections. Then, I felt a tap on my shoulder. I turned, and he said, "Did you just play that?!" I immediately thought he was going to give me shit about it, so I retorted, "Yes!" with no small amount of attitude. He replied, "I love Nick Cave!" I lit up and exclaimed, "Then, let me buy you a drink!"

We stood chatting at the bar, enjoying our beers, for quite some time. I learned that his name was Chris and that despite looking young to me, he was seven years older. I had a rule not to date younger guys because it felt like dating one of my brother's friends or something. Chris had graduated from the Denver Art Institute and had lived in DC for quite some time. I was instantly smitten. It was important to me that if I was going to date someone, they would need to accept and encourage my creative endeavors. Also, he had the most interesting shade of brown eyes, with a happy twinkle that was both intelligent and kind.

It didn't take long for Chris and I to fall into a beautiful, loving friendship and romantic relationship, culminating in our wedding at St.

Matthew the Apostle Cathedral in the Dupont Circle neighborhood, where we found a place together. It was the kind of romance where your hands are always intertwined and you whisper and giggle together with your foreheads touching. We adored each other, right away, and the honeymoon phase was long (and even now, I adore him whole-heartedly).

But Chris had experienced his share of trauma, too, and with the safety of our marriage came the triggering of old wounds that he didn't expect. He survived a devastating car accident as a young boy, where he lay pinned beneath his father, who died instantly. Chris still had the look of a scared, abandoned child as an adult. His entire childhood had been shaped by his father's untimely death.

A few months after our wedding, he began to feel suicidal, like he wanted to walk out into traffic. He spent several days at a hospital in DC, getting help. Beforehand, I learned that he had stopped going to work and that we owed our landlord close to $10,000 in back rent. We decided to move to Iowa into my parents' old house, which was sitting empty due to the 2008 housing crisis. Neither of us wanted to leave DC, but because we were unexpectedly destitute, we really had no choice. Once again, Iowa was my safety net during a time of crisis.

I assured Chris that he was going to have to try a lot harder if he wanted to get rid of me. I love him, and I solidly understand mental health issues. We thought a slower-paced area, like the Midwest, would also be a better place to heal. The city was full of life, but you also had to work hard (and often multiple jobs) to make ends meet. It made sense to us to slow down a bit and heal. While neither of us was sure we wanted kids before meeting, it was 100% part of our plan once we fell in love and got married. So, that dream of becoming parents was also much more feasible in Iowa, where the cost of living was a fraction of what we paid in DC. Our rent was $2,400/mo in 2010 before we relocated to Iowa.

Chris and I were blessed with our daughter, Charlotte, in 2012. This was a truly bright time in my life. I adored being a mom, and Chris found a good graphic design job that afforded me the ability to stay home and care for Charlotte for the first few years of her life. But, as is always the case in life, hard times came around again.

In 2015, Chris was diagnosed with Acute Myeloid Leukemia (AML), requiring a life-saving stem cell transplant. In the year leading up to his September diagnosis, I had lost two pregnancies and been drugged and sexually assaulted for the second time in my life by a man who lived in our neighborhood and had been watching me. I was ill-equipped to deal with his diagnosis, but I stuffed my own pain down and rallied around him. We had a lot of help from family and friends as he underwent chemotherapy and blood transfusions. After several months, a match was found, and he began the transplant and recovery.

But as he began recovering, I began to melt. I couldn't keep myself together anymore, and suddenly I found myself sleeping on a mattress holed up in our basement, cutting my flesh with razors and praying for death. I was back to the paralyzed pit that I had been in when I lived in Rome, NY, all those years prior. Except this time, I was angry at my body for losing our babies, and I was self-harming, something I had never dealt with in my younger years. We learned that Chris couldn't father more children after what the chemo and transplant had done to his body, so I was deeply grieving not being able to bring another Diamond baby into the world. I told my doctors that I didn't want to end my life, and that was true. I had simply pushed my own trauma aside for so long that I was hurting and unable to see a way out.

I made the mistake of going back to DC alone, a year into his recovery. I think we were both in such a place of pain that we couldn't function as a unit anymore. I wanted to see my doctor in DC, and I had it in my head that I needed to be there and under his care for me to cope and move forward. While I did get the care I needed, and I returned to Iowa after a couple of months in a much better state of mind, the damage was done (understandably). Chris and I separated, and this began a tough time for us, where we remained friends and co-parents, but our family unit was no longer.

I blamed myself, and others who didn't know what I was dealing with privately, blamed me, too. Chris was understanding for the most part. He was the one who took me to the ER after the sexual assault. I kept quiet about all of it, for the most part. The police told me it was his word against mine since the drug left my system before the hospital could detect it. I didn't tell my family what happened, but I confided in a few friends. In general, I felt totally alone. I felt like I deserved everything that was happening, so I kept my mouth shut and tried to get through by myself. I wanted to return to our life together, but it was years before that would happen.

My world opened up again as I delved into cognitive behavior therapy, and really began doing the work that was necessary for me to accept the rapes, the miscarriages, and some of the core negative beliefs that I still held from my childhood and the abuse in my first marriage. I began challenging the beliefs that I held, about being unlovable, about being stupid or broken. I used a notebook to record my beliefs and the evidence that disproved them. I did the work. I didn't want to, mind you. I wanted to ignore it all and forget it ever happened. But, I didn't.

This is what rising and surviving looks like. For a long time, I thought that a true "survivor" wouldn't have to deal with these things. They wouldn't cut themselves and beat themselves up inside for things that were out of their control. But, that is simply not true. Fighting back, doing the work, feeling the pain, and still choosing to try, choosing to do things—that is what surviving and thriving is. If life stayed easy all the time and you never had to grapple with grief or pain, it wouldn't be a challenge. I could've stayed in the basement on a mattress, just wallowing in my suffering, but I chose not to.

I didn't make the best decisions during that chaos, but I was still trying. We all have the choice to give up. It often feels like we have no choice but to keep going, but actually, we do. You can choose to smile. You can choose to say hello to someone. You can choose to make lunch for yourself. You can choose to walk your dog. Even these little things seem huge when you're in a pit of despair. That's the secret, frankly. When you feel overwhelmed by something, break it down. You have to go at your own pace, and that means the you that's in that moment, not the you that was doing great a year ago. It's a hard thing to give yourself that grace. I have learned it over and over in my life, and I'm still learning it.

The work I did with cognitive behavior therapy during that turbulent time prepared me for yet another catastrophic obstacle that began in late 2019. I had often used fitness as a matter of coping because it felt like pain, but it was good for me. Unfortunately, I became sick in December 2019 and had my gallbladder removed. The pandemic was around the corner, and soon, my ability to work out and use my body was taken from me by COVID-19. In March 2020, I returned from a business trip the week that the country shut down, only to discover that I was sick with COVID-19. I was very ill.

What began was a 3-year journey of long COVID and chronic fatigue syndrome-like post-exertion sickness that destroyed my previously healthy body. My GI system was a mess, and my body was wracked with nerve pain. A year into my long COVID journey, I also suffered an accident in my home where I solidly whacked the back of my head on a metal beam. The concussion left me using a walker. Suddenly, I was having home health come in, occupational therapy, and physical therapy. My poor Charlotte was stuck quarantining with me. I was too sick to even help brush her hair; we had to cut knots out of it.

After an eventual weekend with her dad, Charlotte (then 8) revealed that one of the teenage boys that belonged to his roommate had sexually abused her. I called the police, and the boy confessed. That year was a mix of illness, court proceedings, therapy, and recovery for all of us. Chris immediately moved back in with Charlotte and I to help comfort her and to care for me in my weakened state. The horror of it all brought us back together. We're still going strong now, 3 years since our separation. It was our individual trauma that caused us to break apart, and mutual trauma that brought us back together.

Tasky: Gamifying Tasks Using Small Measurable "Bites"

The head injury and post-exertion sickness made me debilitated to the point where I could only move around with my walker for about 8 minutes a day. During my recovery, my life consisted of rest, illness, doctor appointments, and physical therapy. I was living a yo-yo where I'd try to do something, like empty the dishwasher, and then I'd be sick with flu-like symptoms for 24+ hours as a result. I started learning about pacing and measuring "spoons."

I finally came up with a strategy that worked for me, which I call, "Tasky" (in an effort to make it sound like a game). My previous professional background involved reading books on professional development, including Darren Hardy's book, *The Compound Effect*. I combined that philosophy with the teaching methods I knew, relating to making measurable behavior plans for students, teaching strategies such as "chunking," and gamifying learning.

It sounds much more involved than it is, but essentially, it has to do with gamifying tasks and limiting them to small "bites" that are defined and easily measured.

Here's how it works:

1. Find an old hat, canister, peanut jar
2. Cut slips of paper into little strips (Cutting strips off Post-Its works great.)
3. Write small, measurable tasks on the slips (There are rules to this. I'll elaborate.)
4. Fold them and drop them into the canister
5. Draw slips out and do the thing on it

RULES:

1. <u>Tasks must be broken down into pieces so they don't feel too heavy and burdensome.</u>

   - Don't put "Clean the bathroom"
   - Instead, put "5 min. bathroom wipedown"
   - Notice I clearly defined the length of time. This way, it doesn't feel like too much. Grab a cleaning wipe, set your phone timer to 5 minutes, and do what you can in only that period; nothing more, nothing less.

2. <u>Always set a timer, unless your task can be done in a brief moment.</u>

   - For example, "Pick 10 things up off the floor."
   - This is defined by the number of things, not the time.
   - For example, "Put Goodwill donations in the trunk."
   - This is well-defined because it can be accomplished in a brief moment.

3. <u>Start with an empty canister EVERY time.</u>

   - Seems like you could just leave the slips you didn't do in the canister, right? Nope. Things feel heavier or lighter every day. You're not in the same state of mind every day. Start fresh every time. You'll know when you are writing the slips if it's something you can wrap your brain around that day or not.
   - Only write things on the slips that feel manageable at that moment. Set yourself up for success.

4. <u>You don't need to do every slip.</u>

   - Do what you can, and when you start feeling like it's impossible to do 1 more thing, pull out just 1 more slip and see if you can do it or not.

- Don't beat yourself up if the answer is no; you are succeeding just by trying.
- Remember that defeat is not even trying anymore. When I need to be done, I save the remaining slips for later that day, if I start feeling "tasky" again.

I know this may seem like a simple, basic strategy of using gradual small tasks over time to create one larger effect (a clean kitchen, for example), but the way you go about it is important. Feeling paralyzed by grief or abuse, anything, is horrible. You feel so stuck that you wonder how you'll ever be able to function again. It's much the same when you are physically ill and can't do very much at a time. Having a strategy like this helps you to get started and helps you know what to try.

When you try this, you'll notice that many times after you start a small task, like cleaning the bathroom counter (again, not the entire bathroom), you want to keep going and do the mirror or the toilet, etc. It's alright if that's *not* the case. I usually don't do things that way. I rely entirely on my task jar for getting cleaning and other jobs done while conserving my mental and often my physical energy, as I continue on my journey to wellness.

I want you to try some of the tasks below. All you need to do is try. Even if you have zero issues with mental or physical wellness, at least try this technique. You'll get more done, and you'll learn a few things about yourself along the way.

Let's Get "Tasky"

Use these slips or create your own, but review these examples so you understand how to break your tasks apart. Adapt these to your own space as needed.

You'll need:

- A hat or canister
- Paper, pen, scissors
- Cleaning wipes
- Stick vacuum

5 min. kitchen wipedown	5 min. bathroom wipedown
10 things off the floor	5 things out of the fridge
wipe mirrors	1 toilet
5 min. kitchen island	clean 1 floor spot
put 1 blanket in the washer	vac 1 rug
wipe front window	text 1 friend / family member
5 min. kitchen table	go through 5 mail / paper items
break down 3 boxes	wipe bathroom counter
dust 3 surfaces	put 3 pairs of shoes away
5 min. dresser top	empty dishwasher
5 min. load dishwasher	5 min. straighten nightstand
5 min. gather dirty clothes	3 min. cat litter cleanup

You start to feel empowered as you get more things done, whether it's cleaning or work-related. As an entrepreneur, I use other methods for longer tasks, but I still like to use the task jar for little action items, because it does feel like a game. It's like you're tricking your brain into doing more, in a low-stress way.

Growing in Self-Love

I've been growing in self-love as a result of my long illness. I am both surprised and amazed by that. When I was younger, it was easier to be hard on myself, to take on the role of the abusers in my life. Interestingly, when the long COVID and head injury forced me to focus on my physical well-being, it wasn't the lashing-in that I experienced after the miscarriages and the sexual assaults.

My physical illness caused me to take care of myself in a loving way. I had been able to rely on my body in the past when mental health was my main crucible. With the illness, I could have chosen to give up, but I didn't. I worked to get to where I am now, not using a walker, able to stand and move around, and able to take walks with my dog. I'm making plans to sing out again, and I'm working on building strength. I wish I could have shown myself love when I was younger, but I am so glad that it's come about now, regardless of the path I took to get here. I'm 48 now, and I can finally say that I'm comfortable in my own skin. Undoubtedly, the way my experiences shaped me empowered me to launch my own business, to believe in my creativity, and to reach out and help others.

The good and bad things in life don't take turns. I'm going through these health issues at the same time as launching my business and growing in ways that, professionally, I never could have predicted. Life's challenges and gifts can come together, hand in hand. Please don't wait to go after your life dreams, because you're also struggling through a difficult time. The bad will come when it comes, but how you react can be the force that brings the good to your life—even in the midst of chaos, pain, and disability. On some level, we all need to embrace change and know that, for our part, we're going to be a force for good. Our lives are ever-changing. By embracing that, and knowing that, we can let go of our attempts to control it and ultimately live more freely.

* * *

I started writing poetry to express myself when I was about twelve. Writing has been a powerful source of personal freedom and coping for me. I've always thought of my writing as a tree that stretches its branches out, with some limbs dying and others blossoming. You never know when you start what the outcome will be, but that's part of the journey.

Here is a selection of my poetry sharing portions of my experiences and the emotions evoked.

* * *

Hungry

I sat cross-legged in the grass in the backyard.
I slid my fingers from the bottom to the top
Along one of the blades.
It was smooth and perfect.
It smelled so fresh, under the sun.
I plucked a blade and put it in my mouth.
I chewed it up, feeling the grassy strings,
Tasting the bitter green.
It was surprisingly good.
I didn't know that my tongue was
Turning green with each blade I ate.
So, the first time Kristy told Mom
That I was eating the grass, I denied it.
The next time, there was nothing I could say.

The Inflictor

In the dark, I lie still,
My face transfixed and flexed as I cry.
I can't let him see.
I close my eyes and see blood.
And I feel it surging in me.
Maybe if I cut my heart out, I'll be safe.
I am full to the brim with nails that keep on pounding.
I can't trust my eyes.
I hate them in every way.
My face is so flexed, it wants to crawl away.
I can't relax. I can't sleep.
I dream while I'm awake.
I hate my heart. I want to give it away.
It's trapped inside me in pain, unable to escape.
I want to rip it out and sell it for a stronger fist.
I want to be the cause.
I want to be the inflictor.
I can't keep on receiving this blow.
My face will crack and slip away.
My heart will come out through my eyes.

Love Like Skin

If my essence was displaced
out of my body,
I would choose your skin
to be my new home.
I want to coat you,
to cover you and own you,
to be always holding you.
That would be my prayer.
I don't want to become you,
or walk in your shoes.
I don't need to move or speak,
I just need to be near you.
I want to cling to you
at all times,
and do it naturally
as God planned.
A love like skin –
all over and seamless.

Dead Year

this is a dead year
we trod along
our feet encased in cement
a deadly drop
with no end

I see flowers blooming
blossoms on trees
a bunny hops in the backyard
it's like a dream
and I am far away
in a black hole
vacant

I wonder if I've lost my grip
I don't know if I can hang on
I don't feel alive
but I know I am
because of the pain

it's going to take a long time
that's why this year died
and I'm trapped inside this
empty-feeling vortex of time

there's no way to make it up
no way to recover it
I sink deeper
with every moment
I can't catch my breath
I feel so much closer
to dying

Afflicted

I'm sorry, but I find it funny
That you're so afflicted.
It shouldn't be that hard.
But since it is for you,
I know that you're not right for me,
Not right or not ready.
Either way, the fact that you don't know,
The fact that you can't see the awesome me
For who and what I am, is unattractive.
It is weakness and fear,
And I have no time for that.

Streetlights Reflected

I remember the streetlights reflected on the dark, wet pavement.
They sparkled, blurry and bright like Christmas lights viewed
Through a rain-covered windshield, when the wipers are broken.

I remember the carpet, moving so quickly beneath my feet.
It was a skipping of geometric shapes.
It had sharp angles of purple and black.

I don't remember removing clothing.
He must have undressed me.
I don't know his name, but I know his face.
I know he had a camera, and even now, it upsets me
So much that my spirit wants to retreat back up
Into the corner of the ceiling,
Where I watched like a security camera.
As he snapped pictures of me on the hotel bed sheets,
I caught a glimpse of my face from the ceiling corner.
It was like looking at someone else.

I don't remember how his body felt or everything that he must have done.
I was turned into a sandbag.
I was heavy and so pumped full of his drug that my eyelids wouldn't operate.
I couldn't move my arms and legs.
I'm sure I couldn't have remembered my name, but that doesn't matter,
my voice was silenced anyway.

I don't remember how my body felt, but I could see what he was doing in
fragments.
His sweaty face bobbed in the air above me.
He didn't have any hair.
And when my violated eyes were jarred awake again,
I could feel his hands gripping my ankles to reposition me.
I find that part terrifying, so please don't tell anybody.

The Scratching

The scratching is back.
I am fighting it.
But I can't get the image out of my mind.
I see myself in the mirror,
with wide empty eyes,
fingers poised and ready.
And I watch as they dig the skin back,
Slow and deep, straight and clean,
like a device, like a machine
that doesn't know how to do anything else.
I draw lines down my face.
And my hands are like happy claws.
They want to do it again.
I want to watch it again.
It feels important.
It feels helpful.
It feels right.

PTSD

stab, stab, stab
bite, bite, bite
I will chew you, tongue
you will not even see it coming
stab me twice
keep stabbing
oh, the pain is like a rapist
stabbing into my chest

The beating goes on.

I bite, and
I feel the clenching and
snap, snap, snap,
I imagine
that's how it happens
like alligators snapping
but I'm still alive
and it is torture

somebody kill me

I want to end

Little Hearts

You found the little hearts
From my bath bomb
In your shower
The next day
And your eyes sparkled at me
When you said,
"It made me so happy."
If I could measure
My love for you
In pink confetti hearts
You would see the sun
Through a veil of pink
Forever.

Mother Earth

I am Mother Earth
New life springs from me
And you ache to
Bury yourself in me
Dissolving yourself
In my soil
To be reborn.
And I will cradle you
In my twisted bough
Sheltering you
In my mountain cave
Bathing you
In the purest spring
That flows from the rising peaks
Of my whispered words
And you will sing to me
Like the birds
While you peck at me,
Nibbling,
And I will hold a finger
Out for you to perch.

I Was That Woman

I was that woman
crying in the airport.
From Boston,
to Chicago,
and home
to Cedar Rapids,
I traveled quietly,
from bathroom to bathroom,
miscarrying you.
I don't know why
I told the stewardess
I was pregnant.
I guess, I was hoping
it was still true.
But really, I knew.
I thought nothing would
happen to you
because you were supposed to
be born on Christmas.
I was going to name you, Violet,
and take your picture
in a Christmas stocking.

I Replaced You

I replaced you with my stuffed bear.
Don't be jealous.
I don't kiss my bear
Or take him around with me.
I only hug him close at night,
And sometimes,
Throw him across the room.

Icicle

I tried to freeze a tear for you today.
It was cold enough outside.
I couldn't get just one though,
So I'm sending you an icicle.

Cry

After we meet and fall in love,
And do all the ga-ga shit new couples do,
I am going to rest my head on your chest
And then, I'll cry about it.

To Juliet on Turning 40

True, you are no longer
That pining, rash teenager
Desperately clutching
The dagger at your breast.
You have grown
And far surpass
The child-bride
Of your past.
You are a wonder,
The embodiment of
Beauty and poise.
Your porcelain cheeks,
And green-jeweled eyes
At times reflect
An innocence, so coy,
Your little girl inside,
But the next moment
They shine with confidence,
A woman now,
A tigress,
And one to be reckoned with.
What could be more attractive?
Although you may still face
Doubts and fears and woes,
Never question,
And continue to dream.
You, my dear, are still
The effervescent Juliet.
But, you're the Juliet
Who knows that,
While loving Romeo,
He's not worth it.
And you are ready
For the next scene.

Breadcrumbs

You fed me breadcrumbs,
And it was enough to keep me wanting.
I thought there was more to come.

You fed me breadcrumbs,
And they were so delicious.
I was afraid to ask for more.

You held me an arms-length away,
And you kissed me,
And I felt safe.

You fed me breadcrumbs,
And for a while, I was sustained.
But the bite-sized samples of you,
Only made me crave.

You chose not to let me in,
And when you were done,
You tossed me away like breadcrumbs
Left behind on the plate.

I imagined a future you, that didn't exist.
I had gathered all the evidence,
But you only showed me crumbs
And then told me I was to blame.

My Little Pea

There is a little pea
Inside of me
And it is safe from harm.
You can't see my little pea
Or squash it.
It's tucked away safely.
My pea is alive and green
And lightly floating
Through my veins.
It is never in the same place.
It is tricky that way.
My tiny pea is not afraid,
Because it's safely tucked away,
Hidden from your jabs.
It doesn't feel pain.
It doesn't cry.
It stays the same.
So happy and so free inside,
Remains my little pea.

Cynthia Height

Personal Branding Coach

https://www.linkedin.com/in/cynthia-height/
https://www.facebook.com/cynheight/
https://www.instagram.com/imlouheight/
https://cynheight.my.canva.site/

I'm Cynthia Height, a passionate personal brand coach dedicated to empowering female entrepreneurs to build their brand, elevate the way they show up as their most unique and authentic selves, and tell their story on social! I'm a Brooklyn girl, living the wrap around porch life in North Carolina! I truly believe that women are meant to share themselves boldly in the marketplace, and my goal is to help female entrepreneurs embrace their authenticity and leverage their unique stories, products, and personal transformations to make a meaningful impact. With a focus on visibility and the power to own our uniqueness, I encourage my clients to step out of their comfort zones and into the spotlight, despite whatever dark moments they have experienced in the past. The truth is, we all have defining moments in life, that's what shapes us and our brands.

We Journey Together

By Cynthia Height

I walked in. The person who opened the door wasn't someone I recognized. It was her, but so much older. In the past two months, she had aged about 30 years or more. The time is getting closer now, I heard in a still small voice.

Was it her voice or God's voice? I'm not quite sure which one.

She walked with a cane now. Last time she walked just fine on her own. I looked at her face, so thin and so sullen. I didn't know what to say. But I knew what to do.

I just had to be there. There was nothing more she needed.

The calm presence of 35 years of friendship. It was like time went on fast forward for her, and stood still for me. I never imagined that life would happen this way. The time was supposed to go at regular speed for us both. We were supposed to be old together. We're only 40.

I wanted her fast-forwarded time back. This isn't right, I pleaded, trying to reverse all that had happened to her.

Then I remembered, I'm not in control of the time.

The time is getting closer now, I sat quietly, knowing. I hated all of this.

I didn't know whether to pray for healing or something else. I prayed for comfort. I didn't know what else to do. I had prayed for healing for a long time. Healing never showed up at her door. Pain and suffering have come again and again over the past 10 years.

I didn't give up. But comfort was the best I could pray for in the moment. I remembered her strength while I watched her struggle. I just sat with her as she cried.

The comfort of 35 years of friendship. The gift of a treasured best friend.

The peace that surpasses all understanding. That's what I felt in those melancholy moments. I suppose I prayed for comfort for us both, then.

The hardest days were still ahead.

We met on the first day of first grade. Two impressionable minds, scared and shy. Not sure about how the next year or two or twenty-eight would go by. In sync, we developed a rhythm. A pace of life no two others could achieve. No words could explain how our two hearts collided and picked up steam.

At only 6 years old, we already knew that our friendship could never be divided. Though not always in sync, our steps always stayed in a rhythm. The consistency of life's timing for a good long season.

The news of the cancer threw me for a loop. Remission, then recurrence, and finally, the cancer just remained. It was part of the story, two lives forever altered.

I sat down at the car shop one Friday morning about a week later after the first of the few remaining goodbyes. I brought *Out of the Dark* by Mandisa in with me. The book had been riding around in my trunk for a couple of months. I purchased it on a whim. The title spoke volumes, though I had no clue what might be hiding inside. I didn't dare to look. The title spoke so clearly. In my heart, I knew, death would be near.

God knew. And I opened it right on time.

I flipped open to Chapter 1, page 1. The words hit me like a ton of bricks. Words I didn't expect written so clearly. Part of our story, right there on the first page. "We've called in hospice. You'd better come see her as soon as you can." ... "My beautiful friend... had been in the fight for her life against cancer for a year and a half."

It felt all too real. Too much to bear in the moment. Words that reflected the real-life moment that I was living, at that exact moment.

I almost shut the book and ran out the door. The tears were coming. Of that much, I was sure.

Well, actually, I did shut the book. It was too real... but honestly, I didn't know how real life (and death) was going to be just a few short days later.

Six days before. I had just been sitting at her bedside six days before. I was reading words on a page that understood a situation I was living in while giving me a preview of what was to come.

I texted my girlfriend Annie... "God is interesting." She understood. I didn't need to explain or send another word further. She knew and understood what was in store.

And while I waited for my car to be ready, I kept on reading. My head and my heart knew there had to be a reason I picked up THAT exact book.

Our story is not ours alone. Even when we think we are all alone, in the hurt, the pain, and the emotions that we can't even explain.

Even when it hurts, even when it's sad, even when it's hard to string the right words into a sentence... Sharing the story makes this life real. Knowing that someone is going to come across the words on this page at just the right time.

Just like I did with Mandisa's book. And just as you may be feeling right now reading this. I know that someone reading these words today will have the same page-halting experience.

In that moment, our hearts will collide in the way they were meant to. Sharing this human experience together.

Life and death hang in the balance. Knowing that our moments of grief and love are intertwined.

We journey on. Together.

The following months passed with the rhythm of a foxtrot... slow, slow, quick, quick, slow... And then, like a well-orchestrated finale, the pace sped up.

Life and death don't give us the timeline in advance. I wish they would, so we could truly prepare.

There's no real way to prepare for that inevitable day. When you can't even fight death away. It takes strength to fight. But fight all you can, sometimes your strength is no longer at hand. The day you stop fighting is the day that you know. You don't have to put on airs. And you definitely don't have to put on a show. The physical body has done all that it can. To hold you upright, with a powerful hand. The body slows down, and the fighting gloves come off. The body starts to lie still, and the mind starts to drift off. It's not farewell until the end. There's still one more day. There's still time to go by. There's still time to say. All the words that you've held on to, for such a long time. Say them before the time runs out forever this time.

I walked in. The person who lay asleep in the bed wasn't someone I recognized.

It was her, but even older. In the past two months, she had aged an additional 10 years or more. The time I dreaded was coming closer, faster, sooner. I could tell.

She cried as she told me for the first time she felt scared. She could barely walk or move now, the weight too much for the cane to bear.

I looked at her face. A sad reflection of skin and bones. While the rest of her swelling to its maximum. None of it made sense. I hated all of this.

I had no words. But I knew what to do. I just had to be there. There was nothing more she needed. That much I knew.

The calm presence of 35 years of friendship. Again, the time passed on super fast-forward for her, and just barely moved for me. We were supposed to be old together.

The time was getting closer now. It really was. I felt scared, too. Scared I wouldn't be there. Scared I wouldn't be able to say goodbye. Scared because I'm not supposed to do life without my best friend. There should still be more time.

I prayed for comfort. For her and for me. I just sat with her as she slept. The comfort of 35 years of friendship. The quiet knowing of what was to come. The moments drifting away in silence.

The peace that surpasses all understanding filled me up like an oak tree. Solid in my foundation through this hard season.

And the hardest days were still ahead.

There's sadness in a day when you don't expect, for it to be the last moment for you to connect. To allow your eyes to exchange a final glance. To let your heart feel for one more chance. The sweetness in goodbye, or just I'll see you later. Rest now, my dear friend, I'll check on you later. Later came and went quicker than I knew. The next day I boarded the plane, not knowing a week later, I'd be on a flight back to New York, too.

The day came unexpectedly... but quite expected. Nine days after I last saw her face, she took her final breath. And I felt like I took mine. The last breath in a world I once knew. A line had been drawn in the sand. Before this, and after this. Nothing would be the same. New York would never be the same. I prepared to say my final goodbye after decades of hellos.

Somehow I made it to Brooklyn for the services. I don't remember much about the packing or the flying or the getting to New York. It's not supposed to be this way. We're far too young.

I laid eyes on her, as her body lay there peacefully. She was truly at rest. Finally, the toll of the disease, the pain, and the suffering she had endured for years had come to an end. In the whirlwind of grief, I didn't feel a thing. Except when my feet hit the church steps.

My pace quickened, and what I saw took my breath away. A white horse and carriage farewell to take her away. A goodbye fit for an angel. The sun shining its light. God took her into her new home, everlasting life.

My best friend forever, my best friend for life. I miss you today and every day. The weight of loss feels heavy. Heavier than you think and expect. I carry it around like a weight on my chest. The impact lies within, and not many people know... or understand... or feel the weight of the blow. But perhaps in a season, you'll feel the blow too... when saying goodbye to someone you love feels heavy for you.

So, set down your grief, a little each day. And know that the pain will someday go away. It might come back when you least suspect. When a regular moment fills you with sadness and regret. Regret of the life you thought you'd know. Sadness of the places you thought you'd go. The grief you now have forever in tow.

364 days later, while I sit at my desk. My eyes are all glassy, the grief overswept. The tears well up and fight to stay in their ducts. My body resists the urge to cry, to scream, to release it all. The hold music on the phone pushed me over the edge. It was day 364.

I hold on because I have to. There's nowhere to run. The grief comes in like a wave threatening to wash away all the days that passed between death and continuing on with life.

364 days without our morning calls. 364 days without hearing her voice at all. 364 days that she's been gone, knowing that I won't see her again. Not in the same way ever at all.

Life for me had been going on. Until the music brought me to a screeching halt. A long pause. A sob stuck in my throat. A lump. I stop and swallow it down, trying hard not to choke. I push the tears back into their duct. Tomorrow... I'll just hold on through the nightfall.

On day 365, the tears all fall.

The tears of suffering, the weight of goodbye. The heartache of knowing. I stop and sigh. Knowing this wasn't the first, and it won't be the last. The grief of such a beautiful past. A friendship that was built to last. Through seasons of life and a distance so long. The finality of death hardly made the miles feel long at all. Understanding you can't just pick up the phone. To hear your sweet voice answer the call. To laugh and to joke, to share a moment in time. The moments are what last forever, but just in your mind. The memories are what keep you from going under. Your time has not come yet. It's not your time to leave forever. But someday, your time will come.

Until then, your life must continue. Your life must go on. To live in part for the love that's now gone. The memories and moments are what you have left to cherish.

The first year's the hardest, at least, that's what they say. You have to endure the holidays and birthdays in a whole different way. Your heart may feel sullen or sad on those days. But you continue along... your journey, your way.

I've once heard it said... in such a profound way... grief is only love that's got no place to go. So goodbye, my friend, I'll see you around. I'm not sure when, and I'm not sure how. Send me signs that you're here with me because I know you are. As my guardian angel, I know you're never far. Send me reasons to smile, and little things to make me laugh. For I'll look for you daily, as I continue to walk.

The walk won't be the same, because you will no longer be there. I can't hold your hand, but I'll hear your prayer. Your prayer for me to have a nice day. Your ever-small voice, your own special way. Your whisper and chuckle will always ring true, you're in my head, especially on the days when I'm blue.

I know that you loved me, I know you were proud. I will continue to do and to love and to be... but not just for me. I'll be those things for you, now too. I'll go to all the places and do what we always said we would do.

As my guardian angel, I know that you're there. We still have lots of moments we're going to share. Not in the same way, no, not that way at all. I'll continue to live until I get the very same call. The call from above, which maybe won't be so scary at all.

I'll be brave because I know, you'll be there at the gate. To say, hey, welcome home, I've been sitting here in wait. I've been waiting for you to join me. I just couldn't wait. I've been longing all day for you to come through this gate.

We'll journey on together in heaven in quite the same way.

Leading with love and laughter, all day long.

Erin Roese

Dear Mama Unscripted
Author & Host

https://www.facebook.com/erin.sykes3/
https://www.instagram.com/dear_mama_802/
https://www.podbean.com/pu/pbblog-pfzbm-105ccfa

Erin Roese is a devoted mama of three amazing kiddos and two precious angel babies. As a homeschooling mom, she's passionate about creating a nurturing and faith-filled learning environment for her children while embracing the beautiful (and sometimes chaotic) journey of motherhood.

She's also the heart behind Dear Mama Unscripted, a podcast dedicated to encouraging and uplifting moms in every season. Through raw, heartfelt conversations, she shares her own experiences and invites other mamas to do the same—offering wisdom, laughter, and a reminder that no one is alone in this journey.

Whether she's navigating homeschooling, motherhood, or life's unexpected challenges, she believes in the power of community and faith to carry us through. Her mission is simple: to help other mamas find joy, purpose, and connection in the everyday moments. Grab a cup of coffee, pull up a seat, and let's do this motherhood thing together!

Overcoming Obstacles and Thriving Against All Odds

By Erin Roese

"UH, Lord what are you doing to me," I thought as I stared down at the two pink lines as I stood in front of a sink full of dirty dishes. My first feelings were not of joy, looking down at this little white stick in my hand. "We need a new car; we can barely fit three car seats in ours now. We need a bigger house; how are we going to squeeze three kids into one bedroom and put a baby in ours? Lord, I was finally feeling like I could breathe!"

After having three kids, all two years apart, the last four and a half years felt like a blur, and I was finally feeling like I could take a breath and enjoy my kids.

Immediately, I felt guilt for feeling anything but joy at the first sight of the two pink lines. So many of my friends and women I knew struggled to get pregnant or had been through losses, and here I was complaining about how we didn't have enough space in our car or our house.

Then, the immediate rush of panic about how I would handle four kids ages six and under. Then, I felt guilty again about feeling guilty about all of this.

It took about a solid week or so to pray and just let the Lord put his peace in my heart. I didn't know how, but he would provide for us as he always did. I was like, "Lord, I guess it's in your plan, and I don't know what this plan is, but I'm ok with whatever you have planned." We started to get excited about adding a new little person to our family and the kids were so excited to have another brother or sister.

I miscarried about 3 months later, and all three of my kids got sick on the same day I started to miscarry. The feeling of extreme overwhelm and tiredness was something I had not ever felt, even as a mom of three little ones. The amount of guilt I felt was one that was indescribable. Guilt, like I was the reason for this because my first feeling was not joy at learning I was pregnant. Then, it was followed by sadness, anger, confusion, and just frustration at the joy that was stolen away from our family.

Nine months later, I was staring down at two pink lines again in the same spot, a sink full of dirty dishes. The same thoughts as the first time snuck in so quickly, but in a flash, were gone. It was different this time. I felt hope that maybe we would be able to have that joy back and I knew that again the Lord would provide. The fear of something going wrong was a new feeling, one I had never felt before, so intense with any pregnancy. But I learned, as with all my kids I am not in control of what happens, I can just pray and trust God that he has it all under control, and my worrying doesn't stop what is going to happen.

I then miscarried for the second time over Christmas weekend, and my grandfather passed away on Christmas day.

To say that the heart can hold grief and joy at the same time is the hardest thing to explain. Christmas morning, as my beautiful, healthy full-of-life kids opened their presents with so much joy and excitement, my heart went in between grieving the loss of this second little one we would never meet. The smiles and laughs we would never see or hear, and then in the next moment, being so thankful for the three that I have. Grieving for the loss of my grandfather, who I couldn't go say my last goodbyes to because I was miscarrying.

My heart was grieving but yet rejoicing in the little things I could find to be thankful for.

I had been through this before the loss, so in my head, I was thinking it's ok, you will get through this, just pray and remember you have to let those emotions come and feel them, don't push them away or you will never get through them. Easier said than done. The first time I think I was very aware that I needed to work through all the emotions. This time around was not as easy to process why this was happening again.

My body didn't go back as quickly to being the new version of me, my hormone levels weren't coming down like before, I was more frustrated and angry at why this happened again and just really, really tired. I remember thinking both times, "I wish someone who I completely trusted to handle everything would come and stay here to help my husband for the week while I went to a sunny place on the beach all alone to heal, rest, and not have to take care of anyone but myself." Clearly, no magic unicorn of a person popped out and granted my wish. I ended up three weeks later having to have surgery to help my body to let the last remnants of this little person leave my body. I just remember thinking, "Good, we can finally close this chapter and move on, get back to 'normal.'"

As I struggled to find what that new "normal" was, I just remember feeling so tired, easily overwhelmed, and just some days so frustrated with the kids and life; the noise was so loud some days. I finally went to the doctor and explained how I was feeling, not hungry, tired all the time, and my anxiety was worse some days. She looked right at me and said, "Erin, you have had two miscarriages in less than a year, and your grandfather just passed away. You're grieving. Give yourself grace, you're literally in the grieving process and need to take care of yourself. Your body is telling you that, and you need to start listening."

Wait, what? Put myself first? I am, aren't I? Clearly, I was not, and my body was telling me this, but I wasn't listening. After she said that, it was almost like a weight had been lifted off my body. I was given permission to put myself first. It isn't selfish, it isn't wrong. To be the best mother, wife, and me, I need to start taking care of myself. I knew this, I think we all know this, but here comes that guilt again about setting time aside for your mental and physical health.

I can't say it is easy. I started trying to take time for myself every day, at least 10–15 min, because I have kids and we homeschool (so even peeing alone is a stretch some days), and it doesn't always happen easily.

I finally understood, though, what I had been telling everyone else: you need to feel those feelings. Let them come, let them wash over you, and then wash away. I wasn't doing that. I was trying to just move on with life, pretend it was all fine and good, that I was fine. But your body knows when your mind and heart are troubled, and it starts to show up in so many ways, especially in our health. So, I began the journey back to the second new version of myself. The new "normal." This meant taking that time to process what happened and be ok with letting God know I was angry at him still a little bit for making me go through this twice. How I felt that the joy was stolen from me and my family before we even got a chance to meet this little life. I began praying and, just in the smallest things during the day, would look for those little moments or spots of joy. It is hard some days to find it, but as you practice, it gets easier. I started to feel better physically. Started working on making sure I drank water and ate when the kids ate and just tried to slow down like them.

Going through something like this doesn't make sense, It hurts, and I know I will never know the reasons behind it until I get to heaven and ask God. But I do know that out there is beauty that comes after the storm and during the storm if you look hard enough. A woman who I consider to be an incredibly wise lady said to me, "I think God allows us to go through hard things because it allows us to have empathy for those who are struggling or are going through the same situations."

I don't quite understand why everything happened, but I agree with going through the hard stuff. I now know what it feels like. So, I can choose to be someone who can turn my pain into a purpose.

I wanted to share a few things I learned after going through this journey. I don't think I have completely healed, but I'm on my way. I hope this helps those of you who are maybe in a similar situation.

1. Even when I felt so alone and confused with no understanding of why God still showed up in my life in so many ways to show me he was with me. My favorite verse during this time was Mathew 11:28-30, "Come to me, all you who are weary and heavy laden and I will give you rest. Take my yoke upon you and learn from me, for I am gentle and humble in heart and you will find rest for your souls. For my yoke is easy and my burden is light". I knew this burden was too heavy for me to carry alone. The guilt, sadness, pain, anger, frustration, feeling of failing, and just the heaviness of all of it. I learned that I can try to carry it on my own, but it is so much weight to bear for my heart. I had to learn to give it to Him. To tell Him everything my heart was feeling and to ask Him to heal it, to take it from me. He did. The only way to describe it was like someone had just lifted a 100-pound weight off of my body. We aren't meant to carry such heavy things throughout life all by ourselves.

2. I thought I was really good at dealing with my emotions, and it turns out, I kinda sucked at it. The first time going through the miscarriage, I made sure I worked through it. It took time for me to process what happened; the second time, not so much. My body started to tell me that I was not taking the time to work through my emotions. I was just going through my day, pushing it down or away because I had kids to take care of and a house to run. Some days, trying to deal with those emotions felt like too much. But processing those feelings and emotions helps us to heal and move on. I had to be ok witht that some days. It is also ok to not be ok. We don't have to try to cover up that we are having a rough day or pretend to be 100% fine. It is ok to find someone you trust and say, "I'm struggling today. Can I just vent?" Let yourself feel that emotion for 15–30 min and be in the moment, then let it go and move through it, so you don't let it steal your joy from the rest of your day or your tomorrows.

3. I could question why this happened a million times, but it wouldn't change anything. I had to accept what happened and that I might never know why until I got to the pearly gates and had a long conversation with God. The verse that kept coming into my head from when I was little and clung to was Jeremiah 29:11, "For I know the plans I have for you declares the Lord, plans to prosper you and not harm you, plans to give you hope and a future. Then you will call on me and come and pray to me and find me when you see me with all your heart." I am completely sure that part of this plan was to have me start sharing my voice and story, which I never would have done if I had not gone through this. Two months after the first miscarriage, I had the opportunity to write as a co-author in another book with 39 other women. Sharing my story, and in that process, I started to heal. I never would have even considered writing before this. I wanted to turn this pain into purpose to share with other women that there is joy after the pain. You will find it, but it comes in time. I also can see how through this, I was inspired and encouraged to start a motherhood podcast. Sharing stories from one mom to another about their journey of motherhood to help encourage them that they are not alone. I had felt so alone going through this, and I was able to connect with so many incredible women, who I never would have met if this had not happened, who share the same struggles as me. It helped me to see I wasn't alone and continues to fire that purpose to share the struggles we go through.

4. People will disappoint you, and that's ok. You learn to love them where they are at and forgive them. I had to understand and accept that people would let me down. The ones you think will show up in times like this and don't hurt to your core. I had to accept that just because they don't show up doesn't mean they

don't love or care for me. They are human, and we all disappoint each other in some way or another. God is really the only one who can fill that space; I cannot look for others to fill it. It also helped me to truly see what kind of friend I wanted to be to others and what type of relationship we had. Was I a friend they felt they could share their struggles with and someone they felt safe to be vulnerable with? I started to see who the ones were that showed up as I was in such a vulnerable state. It made me so thankful that God had placed them in my life during this time.

5. Joy does come again, I promise. Psalm 30:5, "Weeping may endure for a night, but joy comes in the morning." The night might seem so long like the morning will never come, but it does. A little at a time, you start to see the darkness get lighter. There is no set protocol for grieving or working through your struggles. We all handle it differently there is no timeline to say, "Ok, you stop feeling this way after this many months." I had to purposefully choose to look for those little moments of joy each day. It wasn't easy, and I still struggle to this day on those really hard days to find that one thing that I can be thankful for.

So, my friend, if you are reading this and struggling through some hard things, I see you, and you're not alone. I wish I could sit with you in a sunny spot with a nice hot cup of coffee in our hands, and you could share those struggles and be encouraged that it does get better. On the days when it feels so hard, and the weight feels so heavy on your shoulders, take a minute and try this.

Close your eyes, count to four, take a deep breath in, hold it, and count to eight—then, blow out for seven seconds. Do this two times and see how you feel. Then, say a little prayer of gratitude for the breath you just breathed into your lungs.

You are loved, you have a purpose, and there is a reason why you are here.

Loretta Langille

True Healing Ocean Retreat
Retreat Founder, Certified Coach & Wellness Guide

https://www.linkedin.com/in/loretta-langille-bhsc-cec-pcc-69982593/
https://www.facebook.com/truehealingoceanretreat/
https://www.instagram.com/truehealingoceanretreat/
https://www.truehealingoceanretreat.com/

Loretta Langille is a Certified Coach, Retreat Host and Wellness Practitioner who has a deep passion for holistic wellness. After many years of self-healing, professional training and experience supporting her clients; she followed her heart and soul-calling to create a sacred healing space where her guests come to experience intimate solo and two-person wellness retreats. True Healing Ocean Retreat is set in the heart of nature on Vancouver Island in Canada surrounded by lush rainforest and spectacular views of the Salish Sea and Olympic Mountains. Loretta firmly believes we all have deep wisdom within, but sometimes we need the right environment and assistance to retrieve it. She utilizes ancient and modern practices such as: Professional Coaching, Emotional Freedom Techniques, Sound Healing, Yoga and Massage to gently guide her clients back to their confident inner leader, calmness and self-love. She also serves her coaching clients online so support is easy to access.

My Spirit Grabbed the Wheel!

By Loretta Langille

Have you ever experienced a reoccurring dream? I had the same one for years: *I'd see myself sitting in the backseat of a car that was out of control. With no one in the driver's seat, I would awkwardly try to steer the car from the backseat trying to prevent it from crashing! However, without access to the brake pedal, I had no safe way of slowing it all down! It was scary!* In my waking life, I was s-t-r-e-s-s-e-d out.

I felt lost, disconnected from myself and completely burnt out even though I was living the life I had planned for myself. I often thought to myself, "Is this it? Is this all that life has to offer?" According to societal norms, I had what was supposed to make me happy; a kind husband, healthy children, a small but nice home in a safe neighbourhood, a few solid friends and a fairly consistent pay cheque. BUT I lost myself in all the roles I played, such as Dental Hygienist, mother, wife, friend and daughter. I often felt like a single mom since my husband worked very long hours and was less present from his own stress. My job felt like an exhausting grind. My body was in constant pain from headaches, muscle aches and stomach issues. At bedtime, my mind raced and I had to resort to using white noise to try and drown out all the thinking. I realized early on in my career that I needed change, and I took steps to branch out, but with education specific to dental hygiene, I felt trapped. Also, the idea of starting over felt scary, especially financially. I loved spending my days off at home with my kids, but many days I was so burnt out from work, I felt like I was just recuperating before having to go do it all over again. I felt confident in my skills at work, and I loved connecting with my dental clients, but the environment and the repetitive nature of the job were sucking the life out of my body, mind and soul! Looking back, I can now see my nervous system was going through varying degrees of fight, flight or freeze. **I was in survival mode**.

Then one night, I was driving home from work, after another long 12-hour shift, and I thought to myself, "That guardrail is looking pretty good right now...or maybe I should just keep driving." I wasn't actually going to harm myself, but the fact that I had these dark thoughts was a HUGE wake-up call. I knew in that moment I NEEDED change, but I still didn't know what else to do.

However, my need for change was now burning so ferociously that I refused to allow myself to settle for feeling stuck any longer! In my search for what was next, I decided to start working towards my university degree on a part-time basis to expand my options. It was a lot to juggle with work and a family, but **it sure felt good to start moving myself back into the driver's seat of my life again!** I hadn't discovered how to listen to my heart yet; however, I was accustomed to listening to my gut. My intuition started guiding me to inspirational coaches such as Tony Robbins. His CDs helped me start to clear the cobwebs, reframe my thinking and get a bit clearer on what I might want next.

I knew I loved the health and wellness industry and learning new things. As a Dental Hygienist I attended many continuing education lectures. One evening while sitting in the audience listening to one of my favourite speakers, I turned to my colleague sitting beside me and said, "That's going to be me up there one day." Even though, at the time, I was too shy to even ask a question from the audience; somewhere inside myself, I knew I had way more potential.

Then another wake-up call arrived. My Nonna died. While I sat in my Nonna's funeral mass, I thought to myself, "Life is too short to be miserable! I need to quit my job," and with the loving support of my husband and mother, I did just that a few days later. Immediately after giving my notice, I felt a HUGE weight lift off of me. I started feeling more like myself again, and even my friends noticed I was "back." I continued to work as a temp occasionally in Dental Hygiene and focused more intently on working through my Health Sciences degree.

I also joined Toastmasters to build my confidence in public speaking. I turned off the TV and listened to many great audiobooks of other inspiring stories and different perspectives on life. I still attended dental hygiene lectures, and one night at a meeting, I approached the owner of a continuing education company. She gave me an opportunity to become a self-employed speaker. I did eventually end up speaking on that stage I saw myself on a couple of years before. **An amazing thing happens when we step outside of our comfort zone and declare what we want!**

Although, I realized that I was still GRINDING while putting together these professional development courses. I wasn't a very good boss to myself! I wasn't taking enough breaks to eat, hydrate and get exercise. I was still operating in the old ways because I hadn't changed my mindset enough yet. Then it happened. I suffered a concussion that slowed me way down. The intense symptoms persisted over 18 months. During this time, I had to learn how to pace myself, listen to my body and develop tools to manage my busy mind. Done were the days of keeping busy as a coping strategy to avoid my thoughts.

As my path continued, I hired my first coach, and the process of doing my "inner work" started to unfold this time in a much deeper way. I was beginning to meditate more often and started to access my dreams in a whole new way. When I first left my main job in 2012, I really didn't have much of a plan, but the truth was I had known for a while that I wanted to become a coach; I just hadn't let myself dream that big yet.

My continued quest for learning led me to find yet another inspiring speaker, Dorothy, who modeled creativity and mindful living. I once again went with my gut and reached out to her, and we ended up forming a business together. We collaborated on ways to inspire workplace wellness and wanted to lead change in dentistry.

As I continued to pave a new path forward, I still worked in the dental industry as a temp for a lovely group of dentists, but my body was

DONE with clinical work, and my heart was calling me towards something more meaningful. So, in 2016, I retired completely from my 14-year career as a Dental Hygienist to pursue professional coaching. Retiring my dental hygiene license was the leap of faith I needed to cut away the safety net and jump more fully into my next career.

I found my next profession; this time, not by following my head, but by following my heart. Following it more than halfway across the country, actually. I recall as I stood in that classroom at Royal Roads University for the Executive Coaching Program, I felt deeply that I was where I was supposed to be. The program and the connections I made were life-changing and continued to support me in developing ways of being more in alignment with who I am and what matters most to me. Similarly, walking through the forest there, I felt like I was home within myself.

After the training, Dorothy and I continued to collaborate and I opened my coaching practice. During this time, I had a profound dream. *In the dream, Dorothy was telling me she couldn't continue the business, and I asked myself, "Now, what am I going to do?" Then all of a sudden, I heard "The Breathworks," and I saw a photo of a pretty blond woman.* I woke up with a jolt, and I googled "breathworks," and to my amazement, I found the woman I saw in my dream! I read her bio and saw she was a corporate escapee who was offering Transformational Breath™. I had never seen her anywhere before and never heard of this breath practice! I reached out to her (feeling a little awkward: *Hey, I don't know you, but I dreamt of you, lol*), and she replied, explaining this sort of thing happens often; people find her in mysterious ways! What a relief that was! At the time, she was a UK citizen residing in Brazil and I was in Canada. My dream led me across the world! I met with her over Zoom, and we instantly connected as she shared more about her story and guided breathwork. After this conversation, I found someone in Canada who I could practice Transformational Breath™ with. Since it was a far drive, I made it a healing retreat for myself. I experienced breathwork sessions, Usui Reiki and crystal healing sessions. I found I really resonated with Reiki and the breathwork was definitely cleansing and powerful. So, later I went back a few times to study Reiki there. I also stayed in touch with the lovely woman from my dream, and I have enjoyed doing her Conscious Connected Breathwork over Zoom, another wonderful modality!

Eventually, my business with Dorothy did come to a close. We tried to give back to the dental community, but in the end, we were both meant to move beyond that world. I am grateful our friendship has continued.

My spirit now had the wheel. It was leading me towards a healthier career and life. I knew the next evolution in my career journey was to stop grinding and become the person I needed to be to not only care for my clients but myself too. I felt deeply in my heart that we are meant to thrive doing what we love, not just living for a pay cheque.

As I began to coach more clients and receive hundreds of hours of coaching myself (over the years), I came to realize the biggest obstacle is often ourselves. I did a TON of inner work to get out of my own way with the support of my coaches, wellness practitioners and friends. I found Emotional Freedom Techniques mixed with coaching helped to tame my inner critical voices, love myself more deeply by navigating my shadows and sit with uncertainty and fear as it arose as I continued to take greater leaps of faith. To be honest, this inner work wasn't always easy, some days, it was hard to pull myself out of bed and find the motivation to keep building a business. But it was the deep inner excavation I needed. Just like opening Pandora's box, once I had more awareness, I couldn't go back to "sleep," nor did I want to. Never again will I let myself sit in the backseat of my own life. (And yes, thankfully, that reoccurring dream stopped.)

During my rising, my intuition led me to many more people and healing modalities, first for healing myself, and later, I began sharing them with others. I started to build a career for myself with several powerful holistic practices, including Reiki, meditation, Emotional Freedom Techniques and Sound Healing, which all meshed so well with my coaching practice. I began leading meditation groups, collaborative events and sound healing sessions. I loved the work, but it was challenging as my business still wasn't thriving financially. I see now that I was investing in myself through this process. I was GROWING and my nervous system was developing way more capacity. The thing I didn't realize then was I needed all these wellness tools and all this growth to continue the journey towards the dreams I didn't know I had yet.

Then one day, while I was meditating, I had a vision: *I saw myself standing outside a wellness retreat center I owned that was nestled in the forest and overlooking the most beautiful view of the ocean and mountains. I felt deep purpose and ease within myself.* When I opened my eyes, I traced it out on paper, and I allowed the vision to live on my vision board and in my heart. At the time, it felt impossible, and I didn't know if my family would get on board with the idea of moving across the country from Ontario to British Columbia. But in November 2019, we put our house on the market for sale, we knew it wasn't the best time to sell, but we figured we'd try. Then BOOM, the pandemic hit, and some people in my life started saying, "I guess you won't be going now." However, we didn't abandon our plan; rather, it was more like pressing the pause button. In the summer of 2020, the house sold, and we took our boys out to see the island and look for a property to build my dream. On our short week-long trip, we found the perfect piece of land with an AMAZING view of the ocean, mountains and forest. Three weeks later, we made the massive move and drove across our big beautiful country. It was such an incredible journey. During this time, I moved through many feelings, including grief, excitement and fear. After the move, my inner guidance system continued to guide me to people and practices. I learned relaxation massage, and I studied Hatha and Kriya Yoga.

The process over the next two years was a lot. From finding a great contractor to designing our house and the retreat suite (yes, the vision was scaled down a bit) to figuring out how to finance it all. Not to mention getting the kids settled into new lives, finding opportunities to support ourselves and more. It was a massive project to re-create our lives and navigate all the emotions and uncertainty of it all. But with the support of our coaches, family, friends and my meditation and Kriya yoga practice, we rode the waves.

To some, it looks like we took a massive risk, but to me, it would have been a bigger risk not to listen to my heart. The journey had many challenges, including the day we moved into our new home, it took until 11 am on the moving day to finally get our occupancy permit that would allow us to actually move in. Talk about the eleventh hour. Literally. But that next morning, I woke up and looked out the window and saw the end of a beautiful rainbow; we had finally made it to the end of our rainbow.

So, in 2022, True Healing Ocean Retreat was born. A place where my guests come to meet their soul and let it navigate their healing path along with my support. Set in the heart of nature, not only do my guests enjoy the healing benefits of the grounding environment but they also are supported to continue their wellness after they return home from their immersive experience (should they desire this). I now LOVE what I do! It is truly a gift to host intimate solo and two-person retreats for my guests and to continue supporting my coaching clients to live their dreams too! My new wellness app also offers a space for my clients to connect with other like-minded people and develop wellness practices to support them on their journey.

As I continue to learn, grow and evolve, I still work through inner "stuff" as it comes up, and I still face challenges, but I keep going. Running a business requires a ton of time, energy, patience and faith, but when you love what you do, it's worth it. True Healing Ocean Retreat is not only my business, it is my passion, my purpose and the 'medicine' I need for my mind, body and soul. Looking back, I sure am grateful that my spirit shifted the course of my life all those years ago! I'm so grateful for where I live now and to finally see my business starting to thrive, but most of all I am so deeply grateful to work with such wonderful guests and clients.

It may have taken me a whole lot of exploration, with constant alternating between the gas pedal and the brake while I navigated fear and self-doubt. But I finally found my purpose. It's really never too late to re-invent yourself and re-design your life.

Seriously, if you had told me when I was stuck all those years ago, that I would complete my university degree, start speaking on stages, travel across the country for executive coach training, be grateful for suffering a concussion, move across the country, purchase land and build and run a wellness retreat, while offering wellness support to many clients in-person and online; I would have thought you were dreaming!

Our spirits can shake us and call us to rise, and our hearts have a way of leading us to live more in alignment with who we truly are. So, your spirit, too, can RISE despite the adversities, LEAD the way and let you LIVE a more expanded life. If you know deep down you want to make a change, but you're feeling afraid, remember I didn't do it alone, and you shouldn't either. Lean on support, develop a spiritual practice, step outside your comfort zone (since that's how you'll build courage), follow those intuitive nudges, and most of all, have faith that your inner leader is ready to lead the way even if you have no clue where you're headed next. Thank you for reading my story; if it resonated with you or you're looking for support to live your dream, I invite you to connect with me.

Cindy Brockway

Courage Hub
Coach

https://www.linkedin.com/in/cindy-brockway-94838247/
https://www.facebook.com/cindyl.brockway/
https://www.instagram.com/cindy_brockway/
https://simplesolutionssystem.com/thecouragehub
https://bit.ly/CourageHubResources

Cindy Brockway is a compassionate advocate for mindful living, dedicated to helping individuals find inner peace and fulfillment by breaking free from stress, perfectionism, and external expectations. Drawing on her background in education, holistic wellness, and personal resilience, she empowers courageous individuals to reframe pressures into positive forces, fostering balance, joy, and clarity. As the founder of the Courage Hub, Cindy provides practical tools and online courses that inspire lasting change, cultivate courage, and create space for calm in today's demanding world. Through her Boundaries work, she helps others reclaim their time, focus, and energy, enabling them to support and uplift others without sacrificing their own well-being. Cindy's approach is rooted in neutral thinking, offering a clear path to contentment and sustainable personal growth for those seeking to thrive in every aspect of life.

When the Foundation Crumbles: A Journey from Naive Confidence to Authentic Strength

By Cindy Brockway

As a young girl, I boarded the church bus every Sunday morning. For me, the church was a place of warmth and peace. Those early days in Sunday School were about more than just the Bible; they instilled in me a foundation of acceptance, empathy, and the importance of giving. I learned the essence of selflessness from witnessing the faith-filled acts of my community. There were constant opportunities to give and serve. I thrived on the sense of purpose and belonging the church provided, embracing the call to serve others as a natural extension of my identity.

A Solid Start – Lessons in Empathy and Service

During these formative years, I developed an impeccable work ethic that laid the foundation for my career. These principles became my compass, guiding me into the field of special education, where I spent decades supporting children and families who often felt overlooked or misunderstood. Looking back, I can see how these experiences shaped my resilience and strength. However, they also instilled a deep desire to give, often without fully understanding the limits of my capacity—or the cost of exceeding them.

Building on that strong foundation of resilience and dedication, I poured myself into my roles as a mother, student, and professional. Early on, as a mom with two young children, my drive and tenacity propelled me through postgraduate studies and into a thriving career where I became a gifted leader in my field for over 30 years. I loved my profession and was deeply committed to inspiring growth in children with special needs.

As my confidence and expertise grew, so did my reach. I began mentoring other educators who shared my passion, helping them develop the skills to make a difference. On the outside, it appeared as though I had everything together, but beneath the surface, I was running on empty.

The Price of Perfectionism

Trapped in a relentless cycle of perfectionism and over-achievement, I operated on 'autopilot'—checking boxes, taking on more responsibilities, and pushing myself to meet ever-higher expectations. This constant busyness became more than a work habit; it was a way to avoid confronting deeper emotional wounds that needed healing.

I thought I was doing the right thing by giving, but I missed the awareness of my own limits—the ability to recognize when I was pushing myself too far. While acceptance was an important part of my journey, the missing piece was self-acceptance. It wasn't enough to simply accept external circumstances; I needed to understand and embrace how much I could give, when to set boundaries, and why caring for myself was just as important as caring for others. Taking Colossians 3:23 KJV—"And whatsoever ye do, do it heartily, as to the Lord, and not unto men"—too literally had led me to believe I needed to do it all, endlessly and without question, as an act of faith.

The Breaking Point

Over time, the stress began to take its toll. The cracks started to show as my physical and emotional well-being deteriorated, eventually reaching a breaking point where everything I had worked so hard to build began to unravel.

This unraveling marked the beginning of a difficult realization: the pace I had been keeping wasn't sustainable.

I rarely felt my best—not because I wasn't trying, but because I was trying too hard. Each day, I pushed myself to meet impossible standards, driven by guilt and perfectionism, pouring all my energy into meeting the needs of others while ignoring my own.

After years of putting others first—juggling roles as a daughter, wife, mother, grandmother, teacher, caregiver, and friend—I found myself physically, emotionally, and spiritually exhausted. Even though I appeared successful on the outside and was deeply committed to helping others, behind closed doors, I was struggling with depression, anxiety, and chronic migraines.

Weekends, meant for rest and renewal, became reminders of everything I "should" accomplish before Monday. My health declined as I gained weight, struggled with insomnia, and relied on multiple prescriptions just to function. Over time, the toll of fibromyalgia, migraines, anxiety, and depression weighed heavily on me, compounded by the unrelenting pressures of a high-stress career and the sting of rejection in the real world.

Personal Struggles and Family Crisis

As I struggled with the toll of stress and perfectionism, my personal challenges continued to escalate. My first marriage ended, leaving emotional scars that compounded my struggles. Watching my children—now adults—engage in risky and dangerous behaviors brought a profound sense of pain and helplessness.

My oldest son, in particular, faced lifelong battles with mental health issues. Beyond the normal responsibilities of motherhood, I found myself stepping into the role of caregiver and advocate, navigating a seemingly endless maze of psychotherapists, hospitalizations, and treatments to address his ongoing crises. His struggles culminated in multiple suicide attempts and, eventually, incarceration.

Even now, I grapple with understanding the behavioral and emotional instability that led to his imprisonment. At 24 years old, on May 8, 2008, he entered the prison system, where he has remained for over 16 years.

As he approaches 42, I mourn not just the years lost but the hopes and dreams I held for the life he might have lived. Some days, the weight of that loss feels especially heavy.

In spite of everything weighing me down, I refused to let my circumstances define me. Even as it felt like my life was spiraling out of control, I was determined to rise above the chaos. My strength came from my ability to think critically and navigate challenges, a skill I had honed through years of working as an Exceptional Needs Specialist. While I excelled at creating solutions and managing difficult situations in my career, my personal life remained a deep, unresolved struggle.

I sank into a dark place of depression, anxiety, and worry. My health deteriorated further, I gained more weight, and the migraines became so severe that I couldn't even enjoy time with my family or continue working. My reality was far from the life I had once envisioned, growing up in church with hopes for a bright future.

I had remarried to an incredible man who was supportive and loving, yet I remained trapped in my own emotional despondency. For years, I relied on prescription medications to manage my physical and emotional health issues, believing that medicine was my only way of coping. Though I didn't have a substance use disorder, I was caught in the idea that the right combination of medications could calm the storm I was living in. But no matter how many prescriptions I filled, the life I had built was falling apart.

The disillusionment and exhaustion were so overwhelming that I made the difficult decision to take medical leave. In those days, I spent most of my time in bed, consumed by the belief that I had failed.

The life I had built wasn't sustainable. It was clear I needed to make big changes in how I cared for myself, and I realized that if I wanted to move forward, I needed to reframe my approach to everything—my health, my career, my spirituality, and my overall well-being—something that would help me feel like myself again and bring back some balance and perspective.

A New Chapter – The Search for Healing

Framing an alternative approach to life can be daunting, especially when there are so many options out there. Countless complementary therapies, also known as alternative or holistic approaches to wellness, are readily available, but not all of them are effective. Some are truly transformative, while others fall short. It became clear to me that crafting my own restorative approach would take time and deliberate effort, but I was ready for that challenge.

Whatever path we choose to take requires emotional, mental, and spiritual stamina, along with an unyielding commitment to our own well-being. For me, this new path meant considering a major career shift and exploring natural, plant-based remedies as an alternative to the harsh, prescription-heavy approach I had relied on for so long. I also knew that I had to create a more balanced routine to meet both the demands of life and the expectations I had placed on myself. Throughout my life, I had always persevered with the genuine desire to nurture others, but I began to recognize that I had been blind to the teachable moments needed to nurture and care for myself. This next phase of life was about envisioning renewed possibilities, prioritizing my own well-being, and learning to truly care for myself in ways I had never done before.

As I began to take the first steps toward change, I realized how difficult it was to truly embrace the idea of well-being. In many ways, I had thought I had found my "happy place" early on, but as life continued to unravel, I began to convince myself that happiness was a misnomer. When my dreams collided with the harsh realities of my life, I felt betrayed, trapped, and nearly hopeless. I longed so deeply to connect with my inner being in a way that nurtured my body, mind, and spirit, but the limiting beliefs I held kept me from fully embracing the consistent and effective routine I desperately needed.

The motivation to care for myself long-term seemed elusive. I told myself I was too busy with my career, that my health goals were too difficult to achieve, that I didn't have the resources to invest in my personal growth, and that I could always address those desires later, once things settled down. But the truth was, I was stuck—and had been for a long time.

Life Takes Another Turn

Then, life took an even darker turn. In early 2018, my beloved father's health began to decline rapidly. Between January and February, he lost 30 pounds, and his mental state deteriorated as he sank into deep depression. After numerous doctor visits and tests, we received the devastating news that he had an aggressive form of brain cancer—an inoperable tumor. I was consumed by grief. The following months blurred by in a haze of emotional exhaustion as I traveled between North Carolina and Florida, handling estate planning, setting up in-home care for my father, and trying to spend as much time as possible with my family before the inevitable. The stress was overwhelming, and I was falling apart emotionally. Then, just when I thought things couldn't get worse, they did.

In the final days of February, just before my father passed, I found my husband in the driveway, his right side completely paralyzed, unable to speak. He was airlifted to a hospital, where it was determined that an 80% blockage in his internal carotid artery had caused a severe transient ischemic attack (TIA). I found myself balancing another crushing challenge, with no clear sense of what lay ahead. I felt as though I was trapped in an unending cycle of calamity.

My father's death marked the beginning of a painful chapter for our family. Within just two years and four months, we lost him and my two youngest siblings. Their struggles with mental health and addiction had already taken a heavy toll, and despite their intelligence, charisma, and loyalty, they succumbed to the destructive grip of addiction, passing away just 18 months apart. Watching their decline and eventual loss was devastating, leaving our family grappling with overwhelming emotions—grief, guilt, and a profound sense of helplessness. It's a reminder that, while hope is powerful, sometimes it's not enough to change the outcome.

My father's death, followed by the loss of my siblings, marked a cascade of grief and challenges that left me emotionally drained. The weight of those losses compounded the personal struggles I was already carrying, creating a heavy burden that seemed impossible to shake.

Eventually, the relentless juggling act of my life caught up with me, and I found myself at another breaking point. The weight of my son's struggles, my own health challenges, and the endless demands of my family became too much to bear. As it felt like my world—and the lives of my loved ones—was falling apart, I realized I couldn't keep pushing forward without making a change.

Losing three family members in such a short span left me feeling emotionally gutted, and when the pandemic struck, it only deepened the sense of isolation and uncertainty. Yet, in the midst of that forced stillness, something shifted. I discovered that I crave alone time—space to reflect, regroup, and reclaim my individuality. For the first time, I began prioritizing personal reflection and goal setting, activities that had long taken a back seat to my roles as a wife, caregiver, and professional.

Overcoming Fear and Finding Peace

During this time, I came face-to-face with two of the most powerful human emotions—fear and anxiety. They had dominated much of my life, shaping my choices and holding me back in ways I hadn't fully realized. But as I embraced a new mindset, I began to see fear not as a permanent roadblock but as a challenge to overcome. I leaned into a structured program that emphasized self-awareness, personal accountability, and creating lasting behavioral changes.

Through daily routines focused on my inner peace and well-being, I slowly built a foundation for living differently. It wasn't about perfection but about progress. I learned to set specific goals, follow through with accountability sessions, and create written plans and checklists for daily actions that aligned with my values.

This journey reminded me that, despite the struggles, uncertainties, and fears, I will rise. That mantra became my anchor in moments of doubt. With time, I transitioned from a performance-driven life to a purpose-driven one. My migraines, fibromyalgia, and emotional challenges became hurdles I learned to navigate, not barriers to my growth.

The Power of Inner Work

Self-expansion became the key—a practice of inner awareness and accountability that continues to shape my wellness today. By focusing on what I can control—my thoughts, choices, and actions—I've stepped onto a better path, one rooted in balance, self-compassion, neutrality, and intentional living.

I began by incorporating small "M.I.N.D. Moments"—simple, intentional pauses in my day for gratitude, deep breathing, or prayer. It amazed me how something so small could have such a profound impact. These moments acted like anchors, grounding me as I rediscovered my faith, my values, and, ultimately, myself. Each day became a quiet act of renewal, slowly rebuilding the sense of peace I hadn't felt in years.

In those still moments, I was learning to live differently—not with the weight of perfectionism, but with intention.

These daily practices became my resilience routine—a holistic approach embracing my body, mind, and spirit. By committing to this routine, I reclaimed control. It steadily helped me reframe my experiences and thoughts in a way that empowered me. I now face each day with a proactive mindset, knowing that life is constantly changing—and we thrive most when we choose to evolve along with it.

As I fully embraced a conscious routine of renewal, my life started to make sense in a way it never had before. While I know that challenges will always come, and I may stumble along the way, I now have the tools to keep growing. I bounce back faster and carry the inner awareness that no matter what comes, I will be okay. I've finally given myself permission to step into the next best version of myself—without the resistance, comparison, or dread that once held me back from true happiness.

Our wellness is built from the inside out. I didn't understand that in my earlier years, but I certainly see it clearly now. Doing the inner work is essential to keep change from derailing us. This is within our power! We are perfectly capable of making radical changes in the way we address the needs of ourselves and our bodies. It's called mindfulness, and we can apply it to all aspects of life: self-care, eating, movement, sleep, healthcare, and so forth.

My wellness journey now encompasses a conscientious routine of whole-food supplements, therapeutic oils, and very specific lifestyle changes that have been transformative! I've found an inner peace that allows me to utilize my strong sense of responsibility to push back, fight temptation, and minimize distractions in my life so I can maintain a spirited focus on my priorities. I strive for balance and thrive on predictability. Consistency in my personal and professional endeavors fuels my ability to experience personal triumph and give to others.

Living with Intention

In the beginning, my self-expansion efforts felt awkward, and I was taunted by whispers of guilt. I had the misconception that acts of self-love were self-serving and something that was non-spiritual or in conflict with my faith. On the contrary! Learning to love and care for myself on a deeper, inner level has brought me closer to God! Self-expansion has energized my faith and inspired me to be satisfied with my own self-worth.

It feels so good to live everyday in alignment with the values I learned and have resonated with my whole life going to church. With this renewed, more balanced focus, I have been able to become a conduit for helping others to tap into their inner confidence, embrace the concept of wholeness—body, mind, and spirit—and evaluate their options for overcoming unhealthy patterns of thinking and dependencies. Once again—like the eager child I used to be—I'm using the spirit of giving and helpfulness to inspire others to strive for a healthier, more nurturing balance in their lives.

It's Never Too Late to Begin Again

I believe we are fearfully and wonderfully made! We were created and designed with a purpose. We have the ability to encounter an incredibly diverse world in our own time—with our own unique gifts—and PREVAIL! And yet, so many people pour their hearts and souls into everything outside of themselves to find meaning—their professional life, church, family, relationships, and caregiving, lacking the dynamic resources necessary for a happier, healthier, and more fulfilled life.

If this sounds all too familiar, I invite you to get curious about the following questions:

What if you put as much energy into expanding your inner space as you do expanding yourself professionally and socially?

What if you gave up your quest for the perfect life and learned how to enjoy your real life?

You can create your own future by being open to change, being ready for the unexpected, and being willing to SLOW down as needed!

Know that your health is irreplaceable and your inner peace is invaluable. If you're in a place where you need to start over or tap back into your inner strength, it's never too late. Reach out to someone you trust for a warm, genuine boost!

Tash McCormick

Holistic Practitioner Nurse & Facilitator

https://www.facebook.com/profile.php?id=578295120
https://www.linkedin.com/in/tash-mccormick-25923a1b8/
https://www.instagram.com/tashmccormick/
https://www.facebook.com/share/g/12CCfVTuwAA/
https://www.youtube.com/watch?v=s3H4oYRr3D8

Born and raised in Bring It Ontario Canada where she grew up in a small village that if you blinked you missed it. Her earliest memories she easily communicated with nature, animals and people's bodies. This was suppressed as she grew up, although it continued naturally during her nursing career and working 20 years in healthcare. The heightened abilities were reignited in full awareness, after going through her own autoimmune body and health transformation. She is known for inspiring women to get out of their comfort zone and into their bodies, transforming autoimmune and stress related conditions, feeling more freedom and joy in their unique bodies and beyond. She has enjoyed travelling all over the world, experiencing different cultures and wild adventures throughout her life. Now she is grateful to be practicing the freeschooling lifestyle with her toddler, and holistically living a healthy, joyful life of abundance.

From Hero, To Zero, To Legendary

By Tash McCormick

In 2020, I was labelled HERO. Then, in a flash, I was labelled ZERO.

Some of the hardest moments of my life have been the catalyst for my greatest dreams come true.

Growing up, I struggled with unresolved childhood trauma, which led to a cycle of self-destructive behaviour. I lived an amazing life, always adventuring outdoors, and I travelled all over the world, having so many wild experiences. Yet I found myself grappling with substance abuse, ignoring the pain I carried until my body finally screamed for help. The physical pain mirrored the emotional turmoil I had buried for so long. To name a few, I had an emergency appendectomy, was in a serious car crash less than a month later, then I developed full-body psoriasis ~ bright red patches that covered me from my neck to my ankles. I could no longer hide the pain I was in, as it was screaming to everyone who looked at me.

This was one of the moments when everything came crashing down, and it triggered a mental breakdown, which I now call a mental breakthrough. My body was shutting down, and my mental health followed suit. I was shamefully hiding the life I was living with PTSD, severe anxiety, and extreme depression with suicidal ideations, all while working as a nurse full-time. The main childhood trauma I buried was sexual abuse that I denied was actually abuse after not being believed on several occasions. I would abuse substances to mask my emotions from a young age, recreating sexual abuse and physically and emotionally abusive situations over and over, until finally, I had PTSD so bad that someone needed my help, and all I could see were flashes of past experiences. This was while I had already been in traditional counselling for a year. It was in this darkest period that I found the light that would guide me to a holistic way of life.

After exhausting all resources from the medical system for my mental and physical conditions, I dove deep into energy medicine, and I began healing from the inside out. Even though I had no idea what that meant at the time. For almost a year, I was on mental health leave from work, and I never worked so hard in my life! I had numerous appointments and self-development each week and sometimes more than one on the same day. I became sober and completely obsessed with the subconscious, taking every energy course, class, and event I could find, plus a 7-month nature mentorship. I took multiple courses through my Doctor's office, including "How To Live With a Chronic Disease", as I had no idea I would be able to heal the psoriasis.

All while I was in overdrive of "fixing myself" and getting the help I required to be able to return to work, my house was in complete renovations. I had been on a waiting list for a year or two, and then, right as I went off work, they were able to renovate my house. Now this was a wildly accurate reflection of my "inner house" of what I was going through physically and emotionally. The windows were replaced in my whole house, and indeed, I had a whole new perspective on life from both the inside and the outside. They had to unexpectedly rewire my house as I was literally rewiring my brain. Fresh drywall, paint and new trim while my body, mind and soul were also getting a fresh restructuring and colour. The whole house, with all of my belongings in complete disarray in every room of the house, mirrored my emotions and traumas that I had buried, all in a chaotic view for me to see. Then, my toilet clogged, and the plumber said, "Wow, these roots are really dark and really deep", as they were unclogging from the pipes. Guess what, during a holistic session, literally the same day, the practitioner said you are releasing deep, dark roots. Like, you can't make this stuff up, it was so synchronistic.

I hid most of what was going on to people and shared as little as possible, so I was very alone socially during this time. I was so neurotic that I could not walk down the street, and I often drove to the grocery store for food and would have to drive home after sitting in the car having a panic attack for 15 minutes to pump myself up to go inside. When I was in public or around people, I would have "silent panic attacks" that were not visible to others, and then as soon as I was by myself, I would have a panic attack. Every day was a panic and fear of how am I going to function and be sober for the rest of my life, especially in public and social events. I was determined, though, and being off of work was the main motivator, as I love helping people.

Finding the holistic route the most helpful and healing, I ventured on, and eventually, the full-body psoriasis completely healed, among other symptoms. Because of my complete life transformation through natural modalities, inspired by nature and connection to the body, it's been my mission to help millions of people. Starting with you! I launched an online course and started hosting women's circles biweekly, faithfully, to create a sacred space to be seen, heard, and felt together. I even had my first public speaking event at MoMondays in February 2020. Check it out here on YouTube "Full Mind to Mindful / Tash McCormick / momondays London 20200210."

Then, life had more twists in store. I had made the decision to go from full-time nursing to part-time, to pursue life full-time as a Holistic Practitioner Nurse & Educator, creating a full month off from nursing. That's when the whole world was put on "lockdown". Almost all of my family and friends were afraid to be around me because I was working in a hospital. I was always travelling and on the go, so this sudden isolation was alarming. The masks were triggering for me and caused emotional and physical symptoms, including recurring sickness, and I was soon forced to get a COVID swab. I drove myself through a drive-through testing because I was sent home from work and was panicking the entire time driving in the line. I used every practice and technique I knew to help me get through this process. I had a swab once before, which did not go well; however, the nurse who performed the test was very kind and stopped when she attempted twice, and I had a full body reaction, including eyes watering, coughing, automatically pushing myself away, then hyperventilating. In this second experience, the lady was not so kind. She was annoyed, angry, and upset that I was not as quick as literally everyone else had been. I watched countless people drive up, have the test then drive away, like they were driving up to get an order of ice cream, done so easy and quick. She attempted several times; however, I involuntarily pushed her hands away each time as I was apologizing profusely. This increased her anger, saying, "Are we going to do this or not?" and asking if she could hold my head tight against the headrest in my car so I couldn't push away. I refused. I was crying, shaking, this time with the swab still sticking out of my nose. Completely done with me, she told me that the test would not be good enough and I would probably have to come back for another. I looked over, and it appeared another nurse had witnessed the whole situation and by the look on her face, she was traumatized by what she had witnessed. I was still shaking and could barely function; however, I had to get out of this drive-through testing insanity! Multiple people signalled me out like traffic workers. I was in such a fog I had to look both ways about ten times, then finally pulled out of the parking lot and immediately pulled over to compose myself. I opened my car door, and I was crying, coughing, and hyperventilating when a lady pulled over in front of me, jumped out of her car and asked if I was okay. I was still in my nursing scrubs and cap and clearly just pulled out of the COVID testing parking lot. Yet she was THE FIRST person to ask if I was okay. I nodded and she stayed for a moment and even offered me food before leaving. Needless to say, this triggered my PTSD to an extreme, I felt completely violated and many friends and family were still afraid to be around me. I did not feel safe at work surrounded by masks while also getting sick over and over because of the chemicals in the masks. Because of this, I was put on unpaid leave in January 2021, creating more isolation and self-destructive behaviours.

Then, thanks to many cocktails on Christmas Eve 2021, I became pregnant. Again the previous trauma, PTSD, anxiety, and depression were triggered on a whole new level. The emotional stress was overwhelming, I had no idea how I was going to be a single Mom. I was suicidal and too ashamed to tell family and friends what was happening at home.

Given the healthcare system and my triggers with the masks, I was determined to have a home birth. We did, and it was pure magic. The second my son gushed out of me, something inside of me switched, and everything changed. I've been more motivated and focused than ever before. I feel stronger and younger than I have in my entire life. His birth reignited my passion and inspired me to realign my life to be able to stay at home with him full-time and practice the Freeschooling/Unschooling lifestyle.

Having my son put gas on the fire for my lifelong dream of the Freedom Family Forest Farm! A Sacred CommUNITY to OUTCREATE the systems. Outcreating the healthcare, school, belief and ancestral systems and more. A safe space to be our true authentic selves, focusing on nature, food, fun, and connection, enjoying potlucks, fires, dancing, sounding, and embracing holistic health, growing food and homesteading. Why? Because it takes a village.

I hosted a round of Mother's Circles and a few events, including an ecstatic dance where I played instruments and singing bowls, while my newborn was literally attached to me breastfeeding. Now I host monthly Women's Circles, and other CommUNITY events, with opportunities to work with me in person and online. The journey of being a single Mama is a whole other story of advocating for myself and for my son. Perhaps for another book. I am forever grateful and so blessed for my beautiful toddler, who is still breastfeeding at age two, while we are practicing the freeschooling lifestyle.

In a society that tells us otherwise, I'm here to shout from the rooftops that you are beautiful, powerful, perfect, and worthy of feeling joy in your body, your business and living your dream life. It's funny because my whole life, people would come up to me telling me their physical, emotional and money problems, asking for my expertise. So, of course, I feel the most joy in helping Women and Mamas holistically transform their bodies, businesses, and beyond, while building the life of their dreams. Guiding them to connect and communicate with themselves like never before. The body is simply speaking....and listening! Let this be a reminder to reconnect with your playful inner child, feel joy for your life, your body, and Trust The Nature That Is We. If I can do it, SO CAN YOU! Let's release the weight of our childhood and past, to transform the body and beyond from within ... so our children don't have to. Thank you so much. I Believe In You Beauty!

Tiffany Hernandez

Founder and CEO of Tender Heart Ministries
Author & Coach

https://www.linkedin.com/in/tlghernandez?trk=contact-info
https://www.facebook.com/tiffany.lynn.5011
https://www.instagram.com/tenderheartministries/
https://linktr.ee/ultimatehomeschool
https://stan.store/ultimatehomeschool

Meet Tiffany Hernandez, a dedicated mother of three and the visionary founder of Tender Heart Ministries and Outreach. Graduating in Interior Design, she courageously followed God's call to homeschooling and ministry, serving her community with passion and purpose. Through her nonprofit, Tiffany combines her love for education and faith, offering support and guidance both locally and online. As the host of "The Ultimate Homeschool Community Podcast" and through her coaching services, she empowers families to create enriching educational experiences at home and in learning communities. Tiffany's story embodies faith, family, and the transformative power of answering God's call. Her commitment showcases how one person can make a profound impact, sparking a ripple effect of purpose and love. Despite challenges, she attributes all life's blessings to God's grace, finding strength in faith to serve with compassion. Tiffany's heart for service remains a beacon of inspiration.

Rising Strong: Becoming a Better Version of Yourself

By Tiffany Hernandez

The Starting Point

I've learned a lot on this journey through life, but nothing has been more challenging than becoming a better version of myself. It's been the most difficult thing I've ever had to do. Not only becoming aware of the fact that change needed to happen, but actively becoming better than what I was yesterday. We are going to look at the reasons why change is necessary for success and why confidence has to be set through faith in God rather than relying solely on ourselves. We are but dust here today and gone tomorrow. Life is all about the ever changing character of what you become, whether you work on yourself or stay stagnant. If I could go back in time and work on becoming a better version of myself sooner, what a difference that would make.

When you're young and naïve with your whole life ahead of you, nothing seems like it could go wrong. You think you're on the right track and you know exactly what you want to do. Then, after years of lived experiences that have taken you through rock bottom to the tops of the mountains, it's clear you still have room for improvement. Learning how to make those improvements is a crucial part of not only surviving but thriving. This world is ever changing and we are constantly evolving into the seeds we sowed the day before. Whether good or bad seed, the Bible says it plainly, "you reap what you sow". I've sown some bad seed throughout my life, but I've also seen the fruit of the good seed I've grown as well. We have to give ourself grace in these moments of realization that we are not perfect, but have the ability to continually improve.

The Realization

It's been difficult to summarize all the events that have transpired over my lifetime and come up with a conclusion that says I've arrived. We never really arrive. We think we need the career, the house, the car, the stature, you name it and we think that is what we need to be successful. God just wants our hearts to be on the right track to make the most impact, which is the success. Whatever it takes to make that happen is what helps us to continue to grow. We are going to pick apart the reasons growth is so important and why you need it to rise above the adversity you experience throughout life. As I've experienced difficult circumstances and challenging situations, there is a measure of faith that has kept me at peace despite the difficulties. This is the key to coming out on top, despite feeling like you live in the valleys most of the time. It's not what you accomplish by yourself, but what you allow God to accomplish through you. It took me 4 years to get the dream career I thought I wanted. Boy was I so very wrong.

I thought I could handle the career, kids, family, marriage, house and be a superwoman. It all came crashing down on me and I had a come to Jesus meeting where He showed me what it meant to be successful in His eyes. None of the success matters unless you can actually be present in the moment and without losing yourself in the process. This is how growth changes you and challenges you to go past what you think is right. You have to be willing to step out in faith to what God has called you to do. Let me tell you, it's emotional, challenging, and it was like ripping a bandaid off of a wound I didn't want to let heal. The path I was going down would have probably led to success, but my family was going to suffer along with me. It wasn't the plan God had for me. Once I submitted to laying my plan down, doors opened and I could see how God has used my experiences to help me move towards the path He had laid out for me. That is when the actual work on myself began and I went on a journey to become a better version of myself.

Rising above mental health

Being in a Christian household my whole life, there are those unspoken subjects and dismissed struggles. Not on purpose, but it just wasn't the norm to talk about or recognize. I've struggled with mental health probably longer than I've been aware of. Mostly because of the lack of knowledge and realization. I would say it was never to the point of debilitating symptoms, but it was there in the background as I moved about through life. Unfortunately, it continues to lurk in the background of my life after having three children and a family to worry about. As I look back, there are the telltale signs of issues like anxiety and ADHD written all over my history. It's not something that we as a society should frown upon, but unfortunately, there is a stigma surrounding mental health. These challenges, whether genetic or learned, have shaped who I am and how I've managed life up until this point. I am here to be a beacon of light for those who have struggled yet want to make a positive impact on this world; it is possible and you can overcome and adapt!

If you have dealt with depression or anxiety or panic attacks and live with the stigma of being labeled, I am right there with you. I've been in the muck, working through all the experiences and emotions that have surfaced from these realizations over the past couple of years. It's difficult to come to terms with mental health issues. There is such a stigma surrounding these health challenges that many people don't want to be labeled with these issues. It's easier to say you have a physical health challenge like kidney disease or high blood pressure; then it is to tell people about mental health issues. In more recent years, it seems like everyone has a diagnosis of some sort. Let's face it, we all have something going on and it's a reminder that no one is perfect and we all are working with the flaws we have. Don't let those challenges stop you from fulfilling the purpose God has for your life. It might take you longer and you might hit some extra roadblocks, but that doesn't mean it's not going to happen. Keep your goals and dreams in the forefront of mind. Ask for guidance to get there and remember your why despite any types of issues you might have.

It's become more mainstream to admit and share these issues, thus making it more acceptable to be who you really are without the guilt or shame of not being perfect. The first thing to note, no one's life is perfect; and although that seems cliche to mention, it's a pivotal point in healing and rising. Whether it's mental health, abuse, trauma, environmental issues, you name it, someone has dealt with something similar to you. That tells you two things: more people are willing to recognize your pain and sympathize with you and two, you're not alone as much as you might think. Yes, each of our issues is very personal, but everyone is experiencing something. We can use these similarities to connect, share, and support each other. The community you create will either help you heal, grow, and rise, or keep you stagnant. Choosing

the right people to surround yourself with is a very important step in the right direction and one you do not want to miss.

While we are at it, let's clear the air of all the perfect lives that everyone puts on social media. This is not only contributing to depression and anxiety but also causing a lot of physical issues. We look at what everyone else is doing and compare all our problems to what they portray perfectly online. I find myself doing this repeatedly, and comparison kills creativity. We cannot compare ourselves to anyone else. Their purpose on this earth is completely different from yours. The cut apple can be shiny on the front side and bruised on the backside. What we see isn't always the life they live in reality. When we recognize that, then we can create a positive difference in our own lives and focus on the unique purpose God put us here to fulfill.

The Purpose of Hard Work

I always daydreamed about what it would be like to be the popular girl in school. What that would look like or feel like? But the more I thought about it, the less I wanted to be that person. Don't get me wrong, I love being a social butterfly. However, the constant pressure of performing and the maintenance that is required to uphold that level of dedication to always looking and acting a certain way is exhausting and stressful! Now, my goal is to make the most impact and sometimes that gets tiring too. You never really can get away from hard work, but why would you want to? We are called to be the hands and feet of Jesus; however, that looks for you in your purpose will always include extra effort. It just depends on what type of work you are willing to commit to.

Staying stuck in a trauma response is hard, but so is healing from that trauma and doing the work to recover from it. I changed schools because my parents wanted the best for me, like all parents do. It was traumatic in terms of a tremendous change in my life. There was disappointment because I left my friends and a school I loved. I still wonder what life would have been like if I stayed at the school I loved. Would I have still chosen the same path, met the same people, and become the person I am today? I really don't know. Only God knows, but sometimes it's necessary to analyze the past to know where you came from and how to rise above it. The healing is hard work, but all leaders must continue to make changes from their past to grow.

Why Do We Keep Trying

This book is all about rising and leading despite going through challenges. I am here today by God's grace, despite the challenges I have been through in my life. From the outside looking in, my life seems like it's been pretty good and, for the most part, it is. I would say almost all children experience some type of childhood trauma, and it is up to us in our adult lives to recognize it and recover from it without transferring it to our own children. Sometimes, that's easier said than done. As a person who's been told my whole life that I'm overdramatic, I'm too busy, I do too many activities, I work too much, I complain more than anyone else, and I need to stop exaggerating everything, I've dealt with serious guilt and shame, which has transpired to anxiety, depression, and anger.

Could I be too dramatic? Sometimes, sure. Do I overcompensate when warning or explaining to people about something that matters? Probably so, but that's a part of who I am. It's something I'm constantly reminded of and continue to adjust and work on. I know it comes from the fight-or-flight response, and my nervous system could use a little work. Okay, maybe a lot of work. I've also recognized that I'm ADHD, and all my actions can link back to that. Thinking back to a time when I didn't react or overdramatize a response when someone was in danger, or something along those lines is hard for me to remember. I've always been extra sensitive to these situations. It's also the reason I pay such close attention to detail and have been such an asset to my skill set I've needed as a leader. Not all of our perceived negative traits are actually bad. Sometimes they are misunderstood in certain situations, but that doesn't make them not useful. It's planting a seed and watering it, so those skills can grow into your next chapter of life.

What Transpired

I never imagined, after all I've been through, that I'd make it out alive and actually rise from the ashes—juggling life as a mother, battling anxiety and depression, while trying to homeschool on my own since I quit my career to follow the calling I felt led to. Some days, it felt like I was barely holding it together, and yet, somewhere deep inside, there was a drive I couldn't ignore. It's the kind of feeling that keeps you awake at night, tugging at you with a quiet but fierce determination. I knew I was being called to more, but couldn't see the light at the end of the tunnel. I had no clue what God was setting me up to do. Everything was a struggle, from educating to taking care of the house and trying to not lose myself in the process. It was hard to know if I was qualified, and the fear of failing at it, of failing my family, and myself, continued to eat away at me.

When the world shut down, so much of life as I knew it changed overnight. I'd always battled with anxiety and depression, but something about the quiet isolation of those early pandemic days made everything feel amplified. My mind became a revolving door of "what ifs" and worries, and the world seemed like it was spinning out of control. But somewhere in that chaos, a small seed of an idea took root, and the idea came to focus on ministry outreach for the community. It ended up growing from a humble no-name booth at a local art festival into building a nonprofit from scratch. I wanted to create something meaningful, something that could actually help people and leave an impact. But it was daunting, especially from all the ridicule I received over my lifetime. Again, I questioned my qualifications but kept pressing forward. If it wasn't God's will for this to happen, I asked so many times for it to just get shut down. Yet, despite all odds, it kept growing.

In those early days, every step felt huge. There were legal hurdles, funding worries, endless research—things I had no experience in. If you know me, you know I absolutely despise paperwork. Every piece of it seemed to feed my anxiety. My mind would race, filled with "what-ifs" and doubts: What if I wasn't enough? What if I couldn't handle the pressure? But there was something that kept pushing me forward. I couldn't let go of the vision I had that kept growing as we continued, and so I kept going, building something small yet deeply rooted in purpose. I found a few supporters who believed in what I was doing and people who offered

guidance, and little by little, I began to feel that maybe I could do this. Maybe I could rise above the depression that kept trying to keep me tied down.

Thriving Despite the Challenges

It was strange how quickly it all happened, and how naturally it began to blossom. What started as a few little programs and resources quickly became a full-fledged community, with multiple families attending fellowship groups and supporting each other. I began organizing community events, and I put all my attention to detail to good use. Each day, it felt like the nonprofit was taking on a life of its own, becoming something that our community truly needed. Showing me that God's plan was way bigger than I ever could have imagined.

Despite the continued battle of my own mental health challenges, I was helping other parents feel seen, heard, and understood. The weight of my mental health struggles didn't just disappear because I was busy; it's been a constant struggle to combat the issues that I face daily. I've had to continue to work on myself and the struggles that have kept trying to tie me down. It's a constant worry that I might let someone down or that I'd accidentally miss something important. Some days, it's felt like I've carried the world on my shoulders, and the pressure has seeped into every part of my life. However, each day as I continue to do the mindset work and remember the impact I am making, and the work God has given me to do, I'm in gratitude for what He has allowed me to create. This is why I am here to tell you: Rise above and rise strong. Be the vessel that comes out on top with a powerful impact and a light that shines bright for all the world to see that you have a purpose intended for good.

The Recap

As we've discussed the stigma of mental health regarding anxiety, depression, and ADHD, it's clear that these issues are tough, but they don't define who you are. Rising above these challenges takes a lot of grit, sometimes even leaning on professionals, friends, or family for support. Sharing experiences and tips can turn your journey into something powerful and inspirational.

The point is, even if we're dealing with mental health challenges or any personal challenges, we can still contribute so much to the world. Your unique viewpoints and strengths bring something special to the table. Overcoming these hurdles can actually make you a better leader, lighting the way for others. I hope this has encouraged you to see your personal journey as proof of your strength and a chance to lead by example.

Even when you're fighting your own battles, there is still an opportunity to shine brightly, supporting and inspiring others who are going through similar things. By embracing your own story, you are not just growing personally, but also spreading awareness and compassion in the communities you serve. In the end, this shows that mental health isn't a weakness, but a way to relate to others and learn how to rise above and lead despite the challenges. Embrace the purpose you were given and go make a difference in the world.

Grace C.W. Liu

GraceSOULutions
The Woman's Truth Awakener &
Professional Communication Navigator

https://GraceSOULutions.com
https://www.linkedin.com/in/grace-cw-liu/
https://www.facebook.com/GraceChrysalis/
https://www.instagram.com/gracesoulutions/
https://linktr.ee/gracesoulutions

Grace C.W. Liu, an Asian American Speech-Language Pathologist with over 23 years of expertise, empowers introverted, shy, and quiet women to overcome Stagnant Communication Syndrome. Passionate about fostering harmony, Grace helps clients resolve communication breakdowns effectively, enabling them to feel understood and impactful in all areas of life. Through self-valuing, boundary discovery, and proactive communication skills, Grace's clients find greater support and peace with partners, family, and work associates. She guides them to speak confidently, embrace their worth, and create fulfilling relationships. Grace believes that Amazing SOULutions are within reach through clear, intentional communication!

Transform with Confidence: Unlock Relationships Through Empowered Communication 'Keys'

By Grace C.W. Liu

Introduction

Do you ever feel unseen, unheard, or misunderstood? Have you found yourself feeling shut down, out of control, or unable to use your voice with confidence and clarity?

You're not alone. These patterns often stem from cultural differences, generational conditioning, and what I call "communication energy." Perhaps you notice the same arguments repeating, the same phrases being spoken, leading to the same frustrating outcomes. These patterns may feel like they're out of your control, but the truth is, the power to change them lies within you.

When you understand the *keys of communication*—and how to use them—you unlock the ability to make small adjustments that lead to major shifts. These shifts can empower you to be heard and understood, and confidently express your desires, creating harmonious and fulfilling relationships in the process.

Empowered communication is about *you* reclaiming your voice. So, let's dive in and get you in the driver's seat of your communication journey.

Eastern vs. Western Communication Styles

Eastern cultures, especially those influenced by Confucian values, prioritize harmony, respect for authority, and the collective over the individual. Communication here is often indirect, with a focus on context and non-verbal cues. Silence can be as meaningful as words, maintaining dignity and composure.

Growing up in a traditional Chinese household, I was taught to stay silent and defer to authority, which made me more reserved and cautious about expressing my opinions.

In contrast, Western cultures value directness, individualism, and self-expression. Communication is explicit, with a focus on verbal clarity and assertiveness. Here, sharing opinions and advocating for oneself is encouraged.

Navigating between these worlds, I learned to balance my respect for authority with the need for open self-expression, adapting my communication style to bridge these cultural differences effectively.

Communication as Energy

Communication goes beyond exchanging information—it's an exchange of energy. Every word, gesture, and tone carries vibrational energy that can impact others positively or negatively. Recognizing this can transform our interactions.

Each person's unique background and experiences shape their communication, infusing conversations with unspoken energy. Mastering this energy involves understanding the keys to effective communication: words, tone, body language, facial expressions, and hand gestures. Additionally, recognizing communication styles and individual gifts enhances our ability to connect deeply.

By knowing which keys to use and when—including our own styles and strengths—we can effortlessly open doors to trust, understanding, and meaningful connections, unlocking new opportunities in our relationships.

Let's break this down.

The Key of Words

Words are powerful—they can uplift or undermine. Choosing kind and thoughtful words creates an environment where people feel valued. Like a perfectly fitting key, the right words open doors to understanding and connection. Tailoring your language to the moment and the individual shows respect and care, fostering deeper relationships.

The Key of Tone of Voice

Tone conveys emotion and can make or break your message. A gentle, patient tone facilitates smooth communication, while a harsh or impatient tone can close the door. Being mindful of your tone ensures your words are received as intended, promoting openness and trust.

The Key of Body Language

Body language often communicates more than words. An open stance, steady eye contact, and engaging gestures make interactions welcoming. Avoiding crossed arms or downcast eyes keeps the conversation flowing and shows you're truly present, making the door to connection easier to open.

The Key of Facial Expression

Facial expressions are the finishing touch to effective communication. A warm smile or an empathetic nod can invite others in, while a blank face or avoidance can create distance. Your expressions help make the message resonate, keeping the relationship door open and inviting.

The Key of Hand Gestures

Hand gestures add clarity and emphasis to your words. They bring your message to life, making it more engaging and easier to understand. Use gestures intentionally to complement your speech, avoiding overuse that can overwhelm. When done right, they enhance your communication and keep interactions dynamic.

Keeping the Relationship Door Open

When we lose touch with the keys of communication—words, tone, body language, facial expressions, and gestures—the relationship door can start to close. Reconnecting with these elements helps us navigate and reopen the door, ensuring our connections remain strong and engaging.

Thriving Through Connection

When you master the keys of communication, you unlock doors not just to relationships, but to thriving in all areas of life. Relationships are at the core of how we experience the world, whether in personal or professional settings. Being able to communicate effectively—to open doors and keep them open—allows you to navigate challenges, build trust, and ultimately thrive.

By understanding the energy behind words, tone, body language, facial expressions, and hand gestures, you become the key master, able to unlock and nurture meaningful relationships. The more open those doors remain, the more opportunities flow into your life—opportunities to connect, grow, and thrive.

So, as you continue on your journey, remember: You already hold the keys. It's up to you to use them wisely, to open doors to understanding, and to keep them open, allowing the flow of communication and connection to help you overcome challenges and thrive.

True Power of Communication: A Personal Story in Overcoming Obstacles and Thriving Against All Odds

One of the most profound lessons I've learned about communication came from a deeply painful moment in my life—my high school graduation. That day was supposed to be filled with excitement and pride, especially because I was finally allowed to wear makeup, something my mother had always forbidden. But as I stood in front of the mirror, ready to step into this new chapter, everything took a sharp turn. My mother began to yell at me, her voice filled with disappointment.

She told me she was ashamed that I hadn't graduated with honors like my cousins. The words she chose were harsh, and the tone in which she spoke made it even worse. What hurt the most was when she said she should've listened to my paternal grandmother and had me aborted.

That was the moment everything inside me shattered.

As I walked across the stage to receive my diploma, what should have been a celebration of my hard work felt like nothing more than a reminder of my unworthiness. While my classmates smiled and laughed, I felt empty. The diploma in my hand seemed meaningless because it didn't come with the honors my mother so desperately wanted. People congratulated me, but I could barely respond. It wasn't that I was ungrateful—it was that I didn't feel deserving of their praise. The weight of my mother's words and the shame she cast upon me swallowed any joy I could have felt that day.

That experience taught me a powerful lesson about the impact of words and tone on our sense of self-worth. I internalized my mother's disappointment, and for years, I struggled with shame, feeling like I wasn't enough. But it also marked the beginning of a journey for me, one where I began to explore the energy behind communication—how words, tone, and even silence have the power to either lift someone up or tear them down.

Through this journey, I started to understand how to communicate with myself in a healthier way, and in time, even with my mother. I realized that not every moment needed to be filled with words. Sometimes, silence can be a powerful tool, offering space to process, heal, and reflect. This painful experience ultimately became a turning point in my life, pushing me to not only change the way I spoke to myself but also how I interacted with others. It deepened my understanding of how crucial it is to feel worthy if you want to speak your truth.

Years later, I had another wake-up call—one that came from the man I love most in this world, my husband. We were in the middle of one of our biggest arguments, and in my frustration, I hurled cruel words at him. I spoke to him the way my mother had spoken to me during that graduation day, filled with anger and bitterness. And then, in the heat of the argument, my husband did something that stopped me in my tracks—he ran and hit his head against the wall, overwhelmed by the pain of my words. He couldn't take it anymore.

At that moment, I saw it all so clearly. I loved him with all my heart, but I wasn't showing it in the way I communicated. I had been speaking to him the way I had learned from my mother—harsh, unkind, and wounding. The patterns I had inherited were closing the doors to our relationship, and I could feel the distance between us growing. The love was there, but my communication was shutting him out. It was my wake-up call.

I realized that if I didn't change, I would continue to hurt the person I loved most. I had to dig deep and face the reasons why I spoke to my husband the way I did. Yes, part of it came from the way I was raised, from the words my grandparents and parents used, but it also came from a place of my own pain and unworthiness. In my heart, I didn't want him to feel what I had felt for all those years—unworthy and small—but that's exactly what my words were doing. I had fallen into the old saying, "Misery loves company," but I didn't want to live like that anymore. Life is too short, and I believe we're meant to be happy, to love fully, and to communicate in ways that bring us closer, not drive us apart.

That day, I made a promise to myself and to my husband that I would break the cycle. I would learn to communicate in a way that opened the doors to our relationship, instead of closing them. And I'm grateful that I've had the chance to do that—to unlearn the damaging patterns and to build a stronger, healthier connection with the man I love.

Practical Strategies for Balancing Communication Styles

By choosing to break the old patterns of communication, I embarked on a journey of self-discovery that led me to practical strategies for balancing different communication styles. Navigating the complexities of varied communication methods and cultural expectations can be challenging, but I've developed a few key strategies to help bridge those gaps:

Self-Reflection and Awareness: Understand your communication style and cultural influences. Reflect on whether you are reserved or outspoken, and if you prioritize harmony or directness. Self-awareness allows you to adapt your style to different contexts and audiences.

Active Listening: Engage fully by listening without interruption. Show you're listening with nods, eye contact, and phrases like "I understand" or "I see," reflecting back what was said.

Adaptability and Flexibility: Adjust your communication style based on the situation and cultural context. Flexibility—whether being more direct or reserved—builds rapport and fosters stronger connections.

Empathy and Validation: Connect by acknowledging others' feelings. Use phrases like "I can see why you feel that way" to show respect and understanding.

Non-Verbal Communication: Pay attention to body language, facial expressions, and tone. Open posture and steady eye contact show engagement, while crossed arms or lack of eye contact may indicate defensiveness.

Seeking Feedback: Regularly seek input from others to improve your communication. Constructive feedback helps you grow and enhances your connection with others.

The Inspiration Behind the Unique Communication Styles

My journey in understanding communication started with a deep curiosity about human behavior. I've always been fascinated by personality tests, what motivates us, and the way we interact with each other. Over time, I noticed patterns in the way people communicated— not just in the words they used, but in the energy behind their communication. Through countless observations, personal experiences, and studying various personality frameworks, I realized that everyone has a distinct communication style, shaped by both internal and external motivations.

I started paying attention to the specific words and phrases people used, their body language, and how they responded in different situations. This led me to categorize communication into four distinct styles, each representing a different approach to interacting with others: **Fireball**, **Nurturer**, **Diplomatic**, and **Humorous**.

Fireball emerged from observing people who communicate with high energy and passion. They are driven by a need to take action and make an impact, speaking with intensity and directness. While their enthusiasm can be inspiring, it can also come across as overwhelming if not carefully balanced.

Nurturer came from seeing people who prioritize emotional connection and empathy in their communication. They use soft, supportive language and focus on creating a safe space for others to express themselves. I personally resonate with this style because I naturally aim to provide reassurance and understanding in my conversations, but I also realized that it's easy to give too much and overwhelm others with details.

Diplomatic developed from observing people who take a measured, thoughtful approach to communication. They are skilled at maintaining peace and balance, considering multiple perspectives before responding. Diplomats are driven by the desire to resolve conflicts and create harmony, though they can sometimes struggle with indecisiveness when faced with too many choices.

Humorous was inspired by people, like my husband, who use wit and playfulness as their main communication tools. These individuals bring levity to conversations, often using humor to diffuse tension or make interactions more enjoyable. However, it's important for them to be mindful of not trivializing serious issues, as humor can sometimes unintentionally dismiss others' feelings.

Through my own life experiences, including personal relationships and professional interactions, I've come to understand that these styles are not fixed. They can shift depending on the situation, and many of us use a combination of these styles at different times. By recognizing which style someone is using, we can better understand their motivations, adapt our own communication, and open the door to deeper, more meaningful connections.

In my own life, as a Nurturer, I prioritize empathy and support in my communication. I provide details and rationale for each step to be taken, which can be smothering for some people. My husband, on the other hand, has a humorous style. Once, during an intense conversation, he drew a picture of me as a devil with horns and himself crying and snot running down his nose. While this was his way of lightening the mood, had I not understood his communication style, I might have taken offense to his illustration. In the end, I found it hilarious, it did lighten the mood, and we both learned from the interaction. By understanding and respecting our differences in communication styles, we have learned to navigate our interactions more effectively.

Effective Small Changes to Enhance Everyday Interactions

Let's dive into the concept of communication as energy and see how we can bring this idea into our daily lives. Small changes in how we communicate with ourselves and others can make a huge difference in our relationships and overall well-being. Here are some tips I learned from communication breakdowns to help you improve your everyday interactions:

Be Authentic and Practice Mindfulness: Stay present and genuine. Center yourself with deep breaths before speaking; honesty and transparency foster deeper connections.

Use Positive Language and Practice Patience: Shape your reality with positive language. Replace "I can't" with "I haven't mastered it yet," and be patient with others to create an optimistic and confident environment.

Show Appreciation and Celebrate Differences: Express gratitude to strengthen relationships. A simple "thank you" builds respect. Embrace diverse perspectives as opportunities to learn and grow.

Set Boundaries and Resolve Conflicts Gracefully: Establish clear boundaries and communicate them confidently. Handle conflicts calmly, focusing on understanding the other person's perspective, using "I" statements, and working towards resolution. Remember, silence can be powerful.

Be Open to Change and Nurture Your Relationships: Communication evolves, so stay adaptable and embrace feedback. Regularly check in with loved ones, show interest, and offer support. Small acts of kindness and consistent care strengthen bonds and build lasting connections.

Remember, the key to unlocking meaningful relationships lies in understanding and using the right communication keys. By identifying and employing your unique keys, you can open the door to truly remarkable connections. Embracing and mastering these communication keys will not only help you unlock doors but also build and nurture stronger, more fulfilling relationships.

Conclusion & Final Thoughts

As we conclude this chapter, it's clear that communication is a multifaceted and dynamic process—one that goes beyond exchanging words. It involves understanding cultural nuances, recognizing the energy behind our words and actions, and, most importantly, embodying a sense of worthiness in our communication. If you don't feel worthy, you're less likely to speak up and share your truth. Effective communication begins from within, and acknowledging your inherent worth is the key to expressing yourself fully and confidently.

Whether you're navigating between Eastern and Western cultures, adapting to different communication styles, or simply striving to become a better communicator in your daily life, the journey is one of continuous growth and self-awareness. Embrace the power of your words, be mindful of the energy you project, and believe in your right to be heard. In doing so, you not only open doors to deeper relationships but also create a more harmonious and interconnected world where everyone feels valued, understood, and appreciated.

Mastering communication requires self-awareness, empathy, and the confidence that your voice matters. By reflecting on your own communication style and integrating worthiness into your interactions, you can build more empathetic, culturally sensitive, and meaningful connections with those around you. This chapter has explored the complexities of communication, the importance of self-worth, and the concept of communication as energy. In our interconnected world, mastering the art of communication is not just a skill—it's essential for building relationships that stand the test of time.

Danette Bencharski

Danette Bencharski Massage Therapy
Registered Massage Therapist

https://www.facebook.com/dani.dyckbench/
https://www.instagram.com/coopylub/

Hi there! I'm Danette Bencharski, an aspiring writer living in Winnipeg, Manitoba, Canada. I'm a proud mother of one and have spent the past 17 years as a registered massage therapist, running my own practice where I help clients find relaxation and relief. When I'm not working, you can find me in my garden or enjoying the great outdoors. On cold days here in Winterpeg, you'll most likely find me binge watching a show on Netflix. I've always dreamed of publishing my writing and am excited to explore that passion further. Additionally, I'm passionate about personal growth and healing and I'm currently planning to build a retreat center offering hypnotherapy as the cornerstone, allowing individuals to adopt new perspectives and beliefs about themselves in a serene and natural environment. I can't wait to see where this next adventure takes me!

My Love Story

By Danette Bencharski

I'm not supposed to be here. I was supposed to die with only an urn full of ashes to commemorate my place in this world. My presence, it seemed, had become less valuable than the life insurance policy that my husband held on my life. I had started to demand answers to questions that threatened the veil that cloaked his psychopathy, and in short, I had become more beneficial dead than alive.

The first twelve of fourteen years of our relationship were rife with confusion and suffering. I had come through a series of mental breakdowns that I feverishly sought to understand. I would strive to process the pain and learn from it, only to be hurled into another situation before too long that would pull all my stuffing out. Life would demand that I pick up the pieces and stitch the holes shut, but I was always left with the feeling of being lumpy, not quite right, and worse for the wear. I couldn't understand why life was unfolding with such consistent chaos despite my unwavering pursuit of peace. I found myself isolated from anyone I held dear, my daughter, my family, and my friends, but my husband remained vigilant and by my side. He had positioned himself as my knight in shining armor in a sinister world that he had personally curated based on my innermost fears and self-perceived deficiencies.

After nine years together, I found myself in a space devoid of hope. I was suicidal and could not find my glimmer regardless of where or how hard I searched. As a last resort and out of complete desperation, I decided to attend an Ayahuasca retreat in the belly of the Amazon jungle. At the time that I booked the retreat, there was a six-month waiting list for attendance, which was to my benefit as I was battling agoraphobia and needed the time to align my fearful mind with my willing heart. My husband didn't protest, likely because he didn't believe I would go, and if I did go, he would have three weeks to do with as he pleased without having to provide explanations about his whereabouts. It was a win-win situation for him. But I did go, and it would end up being one of the most important decisions of my life.

The trip represented my journey back to myself in perfect metaphoric form; long, exhausting, and sharing legs of a meaningful pilgrimage with people I would never see again. Frustrating at times, and scary at others, but fueled by the resurrection of hope that had been lost to me for far too long. It required four planes, a bus, and a boat ride down the Amazon to reach my destination, and the closer I got, the more magical it felt. Walking into the retreat center, I remember musing to myself that the same person walking through the gates that day would not be the same person who walked out.

Initially, I was restless. As part of the agreement for attending the retreat, there was no communication with the outside, I was at a complete loss as to what to do with the time. I organized and reorganized my clothing, and when that was complete, I would sit at my small desk and stare out into the vast jungle that had swallowed me whole. The air was filled with an orchestra of birds, monkeys, frogs, and insects which only amplified with the setting of the sun. I was terrified to take the "medicine". I feared that it might kill me, but I reasoned that it was worth the risk as the life I had been living was worse than death could possibly be. If I died, I would have done so trying to save myself, and so, I drank the "medicine".

The ceremonies took place in the Maloka, a large, round, wood-floored building with a meticulously thatched roof. The guests were arranged around the outside edges, each given a mat to sit on, a bucket to throw up into, and an ashtray to rest the mapacho cigarettes that, when smoked, were used to clear negative energy. Each ceremony was presided over by three female and two male shamans, as well as various support staff of the retreat center, which all occupied the center of the Maloka.

Within thirty minutes of ingesting the medicine, I was retching into my bowl. I vacillated between terror, curiosity, and awe as the epiphanies washed over me in a torrent of information. Through a series of seven ceremonies taking place over the course of thirteen days, I felt the damaged layers of myself falling away. Each time I had experienced humiliation, defeat, loss, and a myriad of other emotions in my life, my neural landscape was refined to better protect me. But it didn't protect me, it kept me imprisoned. I began to see that the healing I was undergoing was holographic. When my self-concept changed, every trauma that I had experienced changed along with it. I came to understand that someone's mistreatment of me had nothing to do with me and everything to do with their own unhealed aspects. Accepting that one truth gave way to instant forgiveness of a million sins against me. It changed the past, the present, and the future. Before booking the retreat, I lived under the crushing weight of pain that I refused to let go of, swaddling myself in it to justify my broken heart. Walking out of the retreat center, I realized that I had been giving my power away. I had made my healing the responsibility of others by needing them to be accountable for their crimes against me before I could feel whole. The truth is, I was always whole. It was I that had accepted their actions against me as proof of my unworthiness; a belief I already held, and their actions only confirmed.

My re-entry into society was, at first, magical. Colors were sharper, encounters were sweeter, the sun shone brighter, and food tasted better, especially because I was no longer bound to the restricted diet of an ayahuasca retreat. I spent a few days languishing in the city of Iquitos, feeling high on life, before beginning the long journey home.

Throughout my many flights home I was excited to see my husband and to return to my life as a different version of myself. I anticipated my newfound feeling of wholeness to be extended to every area of my life, including my marriage. I believed that I would enjoy a sense of blissful contentment that had eluded me for most of the nine years with my husband, but I was wrong. Seeing him at the airport was jarring. He greeted me with a kiss and told me that he missed me as he handed me a bouquet of flowers. As much as his actions were perfect for the occasion, I felt their insincerity to my core like a gut punch. I was dazed and confused. For many years, I had assumed responsibility for my feelings of despair and discontent in my marriage, believing that it was my failings as a "broken" person that kept me from feeling gratitude and peace in my marriage. But I couldn't ignore that I had felt completely at peace and entirely centered up until the moment we reunited. My return to our family home only compounded my despair, and I spent the next month secretly weeping. I was grief-stricken over the chasm that I had only just become aware of—between the version of me that felt whole at the retreat center and the version of me that had settled for a life of choices that reflected my self-hatred. I grieved for the woman who thought herself pathetic and worthless and small, as I could see her now, in all her self-preserving yet self-destroying diminutiveness.

Although I was overwhelmed with emotion, I didn't fully understand why. The process of understanding was a daily unfolding. I began to see that my husband's words did not match his actions. I started to recognize when I was being manipulated. I could feel when I was being lied to. He had not changed, but I had, and I began to see that the confusion I had felt throughout our time together was intentional on his part. I quietly observed his manipulations so that I might better understand what his angle was. I didn't call him out on them, nor did I give him any inkling that my vision had been corrected. I went about my life quietly, integrating the personal power I had reclaimed.

My breaking point came seventeen months after walking out of the retreat center. My capacity to live a double life came to a grinding halt mere days after Christmas when I asked him for a divorce. He became incensed and belligerent, starting a smear campaign to turn the people in my life against me. For months we remained "separated" while living under the same roof. He refused to leave the master bedroom, forcing me to occupy the spare room. He was unemployed without any source of income, and I was forced to continue to support him financially or risk losing our house. He was on numerous dating platforms and actively looking for his replacement supply, but for the time being, I was it. Our home was also where I had been running my massage therapy practice for my entire career, so leaving meant that I would give up not only my home but the workspace that supported my life. It was during this time that I realized that I was married to a narcissist. Learning this was life-changing and rang down the curtain on the cognitive dissonance I had been grappling with for twelve years.

After five months of separation, the strain and sense of hopelessness, coupled with his persistent love-bombing, proved more than I had the strength for at the time. I conceded and moved back into the master bedroom, ignoring my soul's voice urging me to leave. Four months later, I experienced a complete adrenal collapse precipitated by the enormous stress that my decision to stay had caused. I knew that I needed to leave, every cell in my body told me so. My higher self never faltered in its loving pull towards safety, but if I felt trapped before the seizure that led to the diagnosis, the situation was only made worse now that I was forced to suspend work until I regained my strength.

January 2018 marked a new year and my gradual return to part-time work after being off for three months. It would be January 2019 before I began feeling more like myself; the exhaustion, disorientation, and overwhelm had dissipated to manageable levels. Although my husband and I were managing a civil state, the trust was mutually broken. Beneath the surface of a relationship that had been to the brink and back, the murky waters swirled. Something had changed, and I struggled to put my finger on it. Was he having another affair? Probably. But it was more than that. I sensed that he was beginning to understand that he didn't have the same level of control over me that he once had. He shared less and hid more. He made decisions without consulting me, no longer assuming that I would default to my co-dependent ways and blindly agree with whatever decision he had already made for us. The year before, during a routine visit to his parents, he borrowed $100,000. When he returned home, he delivered the news as though he had borrowed their lawn mower. His curated nonchalance about it belied its significance. He brushed it off and skirted my questions when I demanded to know what the money was for.

In April of 2019, I discovered the second collection of women's earrings. I had found the first collection five years earlier while looking for something else in one of our shared bedroom drawers. The collection held roughly fifteen pairs of earrings. When asked about them, my husband claimed they were mine, which I quickly denied... a lady knows her own earrings. We settled on the explanation that they must have belonged to his previous wife, even though she had been gone from the house for ten years at that point. The explanation didn't sit well with me. I knew I had gone through the house several times since I had moved in, organizing and reorganizing as I did, and I couldn't understand how I could have missed the collection that sat in plain sight. Nevertheless, I moved on from it, until I found the second collection. Alarm bells went off instantly when I asked him about it because his explanation was identical to the one he had offered five years earlier. The hair on my body jumped to attention like centurion soldiers. My internal warning system was activated, marked by a tingling sensation that began in my root chakra and spread through my body and, finally, my head. I thought I might throw up. I couldn't look at him when he offered his next explanation that the earrings belonged to his ex-wife. I knew that they didn't. My mind raced to find a reasonable explanation, but there was none to be found, and the signals that my body was sending me suggested something very dark. The topic quickly changed, but I was left with a feeling of terror gripping my chest. I didn't ask any more questions because I knew that whatever he told me would not include the truth. In that moment, I went from believing that my husband was a textbook narcissist to believing that he was someone far more sinister. The ease with which he could lie was the least of my concerns. I had now discovered that he was and always had been the type of individual who collected trophies from his willing or non-willing participants. His Machiavellian tendencies were unmistakable, and I had reached the end of reasonable excuses that would suggest otherwise.

Three months later, I discovered the third collection, and I knew I had to make a plan to get out. The needle had moved on my predominant feeling regarding my marriage to this man from one of discomfort to one of fear. I knew I was leaving, but I needed to wait for a window to open. Summer turned to fall and fall to winter, and my angst only grew. He continued his extra-marital affairs, and I continued scanning the horizon for a way out. By March of 2020, my resolve to stay quiet was crumbling. As the pandemic crept across the globe, leaving destruction in its wake, my capacity for pretending ignorance was depleted. My husband felt the shift and questioned me about it. I decided that the only way forward was through, so I brought up the earrings. His feigned response of relief was exasperating. He was relieved that my withdrawal from our marriage was due to something so petty and ridiculous but offered no reasonable explanation at the same time.

As we navigated the shutdown, another shift occurred as he started to realize that I wasn't responding to his manipulation. I noticed his withdrawal as he seemed to be lost in thought for much of the day. I was forced to be off work and had decided to make the most of my forced "vacation" while he spent his time glued to the television in silence. Our interactions became a movie set, with both of us playing a part. I noticed him referring to me in the past tense. His commentary took on a nostalgic hue when talking about the things that I used to love to do, wear, and eat. I argued that I still loved those things. It was only when he started asking me questions that started with "if you weren't here" that I began to catch on. He asked questions regarding how I paid bills, where I kept the vet records, and where he might find favorite recipes should I not be around to retrieve them for him. The proverbial nail in the coffin occurred when he began sharing with people we knew that he believed me to be suicidal. I heard him on the phone with his co-worker expressing his concern for my mental health, and when I asked him about it, he asked, "Well, aren't you stressed out?" Days later, my girlfriend would call me, her voice full of concern, "What's going on, babe? Your husband called me and made it sound like you were about to throw yourself off a bridge." I knew then that if a window wasn't going to open, I would have to resort to smashing the glass to get out alive. To make matters worse, the following week he was forcing me to go on a fishing trip to a remote fishing lodge without cell service or emergency services. I knew that I had to leave before I was forcibly loaded into his truck. I made a plan to call 911 to allow me to leave without his interference. I did not want to experience his reaction to having his $500,000 retirement fund (the life insurance policy he held on me) walk out the door. I knew it was the day to leave when in the morning, he approached me and demanded that I take a $30,000 cash advance from my credit card and deposit it into our joint account. These were the final steps to my grave; the plan was in motion. That evening the police were called, and when they arrived, I simply said, "The police are here. They're here to protect me from you. I'm leaving." His response was simply "okay".

I was homeless and without a place to practice massage therapy, but I was alive. I had left the house with little more than the clothes on my back, and the road to recovery seemed impossible. I lived in a camper for four months while I tried to find a path forward. In an attempt to recover my practice, I switched to mobile services, providing massage therapy to my clients in their homes as opposed to my own. I was battling PTSD, and some days had to force myself into my car to face the world. The reality of living, breathing, and building beside someone for fourteen years and, in the end, having to shake off the grip he had on my hand as he walked me to my death, is shattering. How could I be so blind? How could I ever trust myself again? The answers came when my psyche began to relax, and I began to focus on what I had gained as opposed to what I had lost. I realized that my fledgling love for myself that I discovered in the Amazon had grown into a powerful force. It was my love for myself that had allowed me to see what was right in front of me, and it was my love for myself that allowed me to believe it. It was my love for myself that had saved my life and helped me forge a path forward. I am alive because I chose to love myself.

It's been four and a half years since I left, and in that time, I have not once experienced regret or self-doubt regarding my decision. I take full responsibility for my actions, and I allow others to do the same; I am wholly unburdened. I have learned, unequivocally, that the peace, joy, and contentment that we seek are within us and can only be experienced when we choose to love ourselves first. I will be forever grateful to the man who pushed me to this realization, and pushed me to choose myself.

Jeanna Crawford

Ponytail Grit
Nutrition Coach

https://www.linkedin.com/in/jeanna-crawford-00246531a/
https://www.facebook.com/jeanna.h.richards/
https://www.instagram.com/jea3296/
http://ponytailgrit.com/

Jeanna Crawford is a Tulsa, Oklahoma native. She helps busy ladies lose weight, lower blood sugar and get moving again. She found her calling to help others on her own journey to regain her health. In the process, she became a nutrition coach and a fitness instructor. She reversed her pre-diabetic diagnosis and eliminated her heart disease issues. She's worked in the insurance industry (workers' compensation) and has seen firsthand the effects someone's health has on their ability to heal and quality of life after injury.

When not working with clients or teaching fitness, she enjoys spending time at home working in her yard, specifically a tropical garden designed by her husband. She enjoys riding motorcycles with her husband, playing with their pups, hanging out with her grown children and her latest joy is spending time with grandchildren. The beach is her happy place when getting away.

Facing Giants and Watching Them Fall

By Jeanna Crawford

In this book, we're talking about overcoming obstacles AND thriving against all odds. Let that sink in. Yes, we've all overcome obstacles, but did we thrive after? Certainly, not every obstacle will allow that kind of return, but the ones that do, we really need to take advantage of. What an example and legacy to leave to those who come behind us.

When I think of overcoming obstacles and thriving, I am reminded of the story of David and Goliath. Whether you are a faith-based person or not, this is an incredible story with some great takeaways.

One of my favorite songs is by Francesca Battistelli, called "Giants Fall." It references some key points which I am going to borrow in this chapter.

Let's dig in, and I'll show you how to face and beat a giant in life.

To beat a giant, you need to:

Show Up

The Israelites were hiding, cowering, and not responding to the Philistine army that had decided to come after them. David, who we already knew would be king someday, was at home tending after the flocks and herds while his brothers were off to war. David's father, who I believe is where David gets a lot of his heart from, decided the boys could use some food and a care package from home. Most likely, he just wanted word about the fight and to know that they were alright. So, he sends David with a care package to the front line. Yes, folks, the front line.

David gets there, and he is surprised to see that not only are most of the troops just fine, but they are also hiding and cowering. Shepherd boy or not, he was fairly sure that wasn't the way to beat these guys.

David observed while the enemy not only towered over his people (this was literally a race of giants) but made fun of them and mocked their beliefs. How often do we find ourselves in that battle in life? One giant in particular, Goliath, openly mocked them and their faith and vowed to face one of them, one to one, to determine the outcome of the battle. Now, David was thinking, "What's the problem, guys, send someone out." But no one was brave enough to face Goliath alone.

David knew he was not alone. He went up against a lion to protect his herd and won. He went up against a bear to protect his herd and won. While the circumstances were different, he knew he wasn't alone, and if no one else answered the call, he would do it himself. After all, he already had a great winning record, and he was to be the next king of Israel.

It takes courage to show up. This kid was going to the front line of battle, that alone is scary. He went with no question. He observed when he got there, gathered data, and then realized no one was willing to stand in front of this guy. So, he showed up.

Where do you need to show up in your battles? Are you hiding, avoiding, or doing anything but staring fear and battles in the face? If it's time to show up for something you've been facing, remember, if a shepherd boy can do it, so can you.

Step Up

Without any finger-pointing, no shifting responsibility, and owning a situation he was not qualified (technically) to take on, David stepped up. He told the king and the troops that he would take the giant on himself. He knew God would be with him, and he felt certain that this was his path.

He was laughed at, ridiculed, and told that he would never succeed. Even his brothers did not support him in this decision. No one believed that he could do it. But David knew, and he was not going to stand down on this.

How many times do we show up and then step up, and no one believes in us? It's happened to me, and I have no doubt that it's happened to many others as well. Step up anyway. If it's in your heart, it's there for a reason. God, the Universe, whoever or whatever you believe in, does not place something in your heart and light a fire in your belly for you to not answer the call. Step up, you'll be glad you did.

Back Up

After a lot of discussion, head scratching, and finally concluding that no one else was going to go up against this big dude, David was given the green light. He must have really been young because his first response was, "Great, I'll be right back." Am I right parents?

David was wise beyond his years. While his initial goal was to get what he needed, he also took the time to focus, reflect, and get in touch with his faith and his roots.

How often do you take time to go to the brook, spend some quiet time in reflection, talk to your Creator, or just meditate? Are your battles not worth your focus? Aren't you worth the quiet time it takes to recharge, regroup, and come back stronger and centered? My friend, you absolutely are. So, in the midst of battles or obstacles, go to the brook. Listen. Rest. Look in the mirror. Get real about what you are fixing to overcome.

Load Up

The time at the brook wasn't just some "me time," which there's nothing wrong with that and I think we can all agree that we need more of that. This was about preparation.

A little background here if you will bear with me. A shepherd can only travel with what he can carry while looking out after a flock. While you might be thinking that they can load up, keep in mind that herding sheep is very hands-on. Sheep are not the brightest, you know? And we're talking about a time with no canned goods, so yes, he is hunting for his food if the herd is far enough out, and yes, he would stay with the herd. It was too dangerous at night to leave them alone. So, a typical shepherd was carrying things like a knife, slingshot, bows, and arrows if they had those, something for warmth, and a canteen for fresh water in the event that wasn't available.

Keep in mind, if anything happened to one of the sheep, the shepherd's job was to return the flock to the main barn or property and carry an injured sheep or as many injured sheep as they could in an attempt to bring them back to save them. Any idea how much a sheep weighs? It's like carrying your 4-year-old, indefinitely.

Weapons had to be light and small, this resulted in his skills with the slingshot and knife. Perhaps a bow and arrow if that was a luxury. Remember, everything back then was handmade.

David was on a mission to fellowship and minister to his brothers through connection, food, and bringing their father's love. Carrying the goods Dad sent and something to keep warm left him with not much room for much more than the slingshot.

Are we carrying too much? Are we trying to do things harder rather than smarter? Do we need to lay some things down? Maybe we need to load up on what serves us best rather than what others think we need to have.

Five stones, that's what he picked up. Not just any stones, they had to be a certain size and weight and be smooth. This shepherd knew what he was doing, and he had to be selective. The stone had a purpose and a mission, just like the man who was going to sling it.

To put this in perspective, Goliath had full armor. He was covered from head to toe as much as was possible for this time period in history. For the Philistines who preferred to live in battle, this was, at that time, a perfect battle protection system. While they tried to provide David with similar armor, he was too small for it, it was too heavy and cumbersome for what he needed to do. Yes, he went out there, barely protected, still willing to fight.

We need to protect ourselves and be smart in life and in business. But can we admit that sometimes we try to protect ourselves from everything and, by doing so, do not get anything done? Could that create us not being in the right spot to move forward? Let that sink in a bit. I am not talking about reckless risks. David knew the risks; this was his life and the lives of his people. He also knew that he could not fight with too much on him. What do you need to lay down?

Wind Up

If you haven't gathered by now, things in this young man's life were getting pretty intense. He came to see his brothers, bring them a message from their dad, break some bread and come back home and let dad know how they were. But now, he was in the fight of his life, not only for himself but for his nation. His NATION. Yes, the stakes and results of this battle had those kinds of results.

But doing the right things creates momentum, and David knew this. He had found favor, he was the anointed future king of Israel, he had past wins already that most would consider to be impossible and thus a confidence that no one in his nation or tribe had to face this enemy.

So, the stone went in the sling, the eyes closed, his heart opened, and he delivered. The one and only spot where he could have hit the giant with any kind of impact, he nailed with absolute accuracy. The giant fell, Israel was saved, and David would go on to be king someday.

How's your windup? Do you practice it? Do you have the confidence to follow through? Can you pull that trigger even if the possible outcome is a failure? Remember, he had four more stones, just in case.

Rise Up

That giant fell, and he fell hard. Once he hit the ground David did not stop there. He took Goliath's sword and cut his head off. Now back in the day, that action meant a lot of things. But remember, we're talking about a shepherd. While he was strong, he was probably not a giant sword strong. Regardless, he got it done because nothing says defeat like losing a head.

Now, we're not cutting off heads these days and thank goodness! Gross! We're also most likely not facing mortal enemies. But we have our battles. Life is not always kind. Our dreams don't just float out of our heads like unicorns and fly over rainbows with the prince in our pocket with a happy ending.

We have to work; we have to fight. If I could convey anything to you here, it's get it done, victory is 5 stones away.

"Giants Fall," the song, says, "Step into the fight, He's right there by your side, the stones inside your hand might be small but watch the giants fall." That's powerful stuff there, I hope you take that with you.

My Giants

You might be wondering what, if any, giants I have faced. Happy to share that with you. These are the giants that have taken one, or more, stones to defeat.

Depression

I knew about depression growing up. I just didn't know what it looked and felt like. Unfortunately, because of that, I fought with that beast way too long.

I've been able to control this most of my adult life with exercise. Later in life, it took nutrition and exercise (which it should have anyway), but it's manageable most of the time. However, there have been times in my life when I have needed assistance with this. If you need help, get it. Medication doesn't have to be forever, and if it's the lifeline that you need, take it. I have never stayed on meds too long, and it was always worth getting the boost I needed when I needed it.

Depression, for some, is a lifelong giant. I have had many battles. So far, thankfully, I've won them all. Do not face this giant alone. It's a worthy opponent. If you ever need help or want to talk to someone about this, please reach out to me through my contact information. I will always be happy to help anyone facing this in any way that I can. I can't treat it, but I can point you in the right direction and listen and care.

Weight and Pre-Diabetes

I was active as a kid and a teenager and never had issues with my weight. After my second baby, that was a different story. Keep in mind, that's when the first round of depression came into my life, so I was fighting on multiple fronts.

As far as weight loss goes, I've always been able to lose and get back to where I needed to be if and when I wanted to. The key part of that is "want to."

Fast forward to my late 40s and that was a different ball game. I thought I had been eating mostly well, I was exercising but not losing. Then bam, one day, I woke up not only with the middle of myself bigger than I wanted, but it was hard. Not chiseled abs hard but way too round and just hard like heart disease hard.

Sure enough, after extensive blood work with a holistic doctor (which I highly recommend, by the way), I found out I was pre-diabetic and had heart disease markers lit up like Christmas.

While I sort of understood the chemical imbalance that causes depression, this giant, well, I'm not going to lie: This one made me mad.

First, I knew better, or at least I thought I did. Second, why? Yep, stayed on that for a while. Bottom line, the series of choices I had made up to that point in my life had put me there, and I had no one to blame but myself. That did not stop my temper tantrum when I found out, but it did guide me to becoming a nutrition coach and fitness instructor.

I am still human. I still make good choices. I still make bad choices. But my health has remained. This is another area that I am more than happy to help you with if you'd like to connect. Please reach out to me.

Divorce

Yes, like so many others, this is a giant I faced in my life. I rushed into marriage, facing the giant of teenage pregnancy. I had it in my head that this would work, but what I was really doing was trying to escape what I thought was pain and disappointment from others. Truth was, it was my pain and my disappointment that I was running from. Regardless, no one is perfect, and while I do not take the bond of marriage lightly (yes, I remarried many years later), we all make mistakes. Grace and love will get you through this one. However, I strongly recommend a lot of introspection, review, and getting to know yourself before you move forward.

Job Loss

Losing a job can be devastating, especially if you don't see it coming. Even when you do, it can be hard to close a chapter and move on to a new one, regardless of the benefits you believe will be there for you. And sometimes, something happens in your job where you have to make decisions that you wouldn't be making and certainly didn't plan to at that time.

I walked away from a job once due to a conflict in integrity. It wasn't necessarily who was right; it was that it wasn't right for me, nor did the situation line up with my values. While it was the right thing to do for me, it severely impacted my income and depleted my savings. Replacing that salary took many years. I almost lost everything I owned through that time of my life.

But I also learned that the little things do matter. I spent quality time with my kids, not just time folks, quality teaching, talking, dreaming, and connecting time. I learned a lot about myself, and I even wrote a few songs.

I'm now exactly where I wanted to be in my career, which just blows my mind. Stay the course, stay true to yourself, and things will happen for you.

Business

My current giant in life is getting my business set up to be my full-time gig. This isn't for the weak, for sure. I have failed, failed again, and kept learning from those failures. I believe that I have a message for the world and need to help others through the rest of my days here on this planet. Just because I'm not where I want to be with my business does not mean I shouldn't pursue it. I've watched doors open, information come when it was needed, training showed up at just the right time, and my mentorship and friendship continue to develop to support the transition I'm working on.

If you have a dream, a passion, or a fire in your belly for something, remember, it's there for a reason. The path will not look the way that you think it should. In fact, it could be wildly different. You are here for a reason, let your light shine and trust that the path will unfold because it will.

Be a Shepherd Boy

If a shepherd boy can take down a giant, certainly, we can have faith that we can do and accomplish what we are here to do as well. There is another song I really like called "Shepherd Boy," so I'll leave you with this phrase from the song, "When others see a shepherd boy, God may see a king."

Go be that king, go be that queen, go accomplish what you're here to do in this world. We need you; you need you, be the best you ever!

Jeanna Crawford

DK Hillard

DK Hillard Art, LLC
Artist, Designer, Author & Founder

https://www.facebook.com/dkhillardart/
https://www.instagram.com/dkhillard/
https://www.dkhillard.com
https://www.dkhillardart.com

Debra is a creator. It is how she lives and what she does in her work. Her art has been a consistent thread throughout her life, whether it be painting, writing or working with others. It is based in her spiritual journey, her Shamanic practice and her connection to nature.

For 20 years she was a life coach and personal trainer, a career that evolved out of her experience transforming her life through bodybuilding. During that time she developed a 12 week program using the body as a vehicle for transforming your entire life.

She transforms her paintings into sensual, luxurious fabrics-clothing, blankets and pillows called "Wraptures", bringing the energy of her artwork into forms you can touch. They are filled with the love that she puts into everything she creates. She works with individuals and small groups using many of the interactive processes she developed while teaching her program.

Our Words Have Power

By DK Hillard

Our words have the power to change the course of our lives. It is not the circumstances we find ourselves in, rather what we say about them that creates our reality. I am living proof that this is true.

I cannot think of a time in my life when being resilient wasn't required. As a child, I felt unwanted and unloved—it seemed trauma, heartbreak and loss were the story of my life from the very beginning. But that has never been the truth of who I am; it was simply the circumstances I was born into and provided the lessons I was here to learn.

For the longest time, my words confirmed that I was unworthy of anything good, that I was the bad seed my family told me I was. Believing them drew to me the people and the circumstances to prove them right. Their words defined my reality, setting the tone for a lifetime of loss, heartbreak, trauma and abuse. Illness and debilitation came along with those beliefs, running through my life in various forms, beginning in young adulthood.

The first real challenge began in my mid-twenties when I became bedridden with chronic fatigue. Years of doctors and tests and good old-fashioned Western medicine revealed nothing. I was told I was crazy and needed a shrink. Nearing forty, with even alternative physicians telling me that I would never lead a normal life again, I made a declaration. I said the words that changed the course of my life forever: "I am not a sick person. I am a strong, healthy person with some physical issues to deal with, and if I am ever to have a life again, I need my physical strength back."

In an abusive marriage and with a young son to care for, I gathered my resources and found a strength coach from a local university. His name was Jim. Although neither of us knew what it would take to build strength in someone with CFS, we stepped into the gym with our hopes and intentions high.

On our first day in the gym, he asked me to do a push-up. I couldn't get off the floor. Dressed in bulky sweats to hide my out-of-shape body, I crawled to a bench to help myself up. He put me on the leg extension machine with a light weight. I did one set. That was it for the next couple of weeks; one set had put me in bed, unable to function. I remember lying there with barely the strength to breathe.

But we had an agreement and a commitment: Once I was able to get up, I'd call him, and we'd go at it again. And I did.

Over the course of months, one set at a time. I made it to a few sets, then a few exercises, and then about eight months later, to a whole workout. I had been training so consistently for weeks that Jim told me it was probably time to take a break. Others in the gym had been noticing the changes in me and were asking me for advice, not just about training, but about their lives. Women were approaching me in the locker room, pouring out their hearts and turning to me for guidance. It was more than my workouts that had caught their attention. It was the fact that I had totally shifted my reality by declaring it so. The strength I said I had was evident now, both in the power I exhibited in the gym and in how I was living my life.

I remember the day about nine or ten months into our training regimen. I was sitting on a bench waiting to do a set of cable crossovers when the realization hit me. I turned to Jim and said, "I know what I need to do with the rest of my life. I am going to be a trainer. This has given me my life back, and I need to share that with others."

It was clear as day. That set me on a course of study, certification and eventually starting my own training business. I was working out like a champion, and the fatigue was gone. I was 40 years old. The doctors had all said it was impossible—I said otherwise.

But that was only the beginning.

At the time, I was in business with my ex-husband. We were both artists, but I had stopped painting years ago to run our business and raise our son. My ex had convinced me that I wasn't really an artist and had dismissed my creative work. Ever since childhood, my family had judged my artistic gifts as unworthy, so his dismissal was merely validation that they had been right.

I turned my focus on our business, and my efforts made it a success. But the recession of the 80s hit, and we wound up losing it all to bankruptcy.

I started over again, taking on multiple roles from packing boxes to marketing, and running back and forth to the gym in between. My ex refused to put in the work in both our marriage and our business. Both were failing.

I told him I'd give it another try, but we needed a change, a big one. So, we moved from New England to Arizona and a whole new life. We would be leaving just about everything behind for the possibility of a new start.

It was the early 90s. My physical strength was increasing as well as my resolve to make a life for us. I wasn't going to give up on my family. Occasionally, I had a relapse of CFS. With each one, as I lay in bed, I had to make a conscious choice of whether to live or let myself go. The choices were that stark—the illness was so debilitating. But I always knew who I was, and it wasn't a sick person. I've known ever since childhood that I was here for some "reason," and I kept that light burning deep in my gut even when everything outside of me tried to extinguish it.

It was February of 2000, and my mother had come for a visit. My father had died a few years prior, and this was our first time to really be together. One afternoon we were running errands when a white SUV ran a red light and demolished my car. It was as if time slowed to a crawl as I experienced the crash. My right arm automatically turned the wheel as far to the left as possible in an impossible attempt to avoid the collision. The airbags deployed, and I heard the bones in my arm splinter. I remember screaming and seeing my mother's head smash into the car door. At the same time, I had an eerie awareness that this was a gift, and it was here to help me in some way.

In the hospital, they told me that my arm was so badly broken that I would need surgery the next day. I was in shock, worried about my mother and feeling terrified for my family's survival. As much as I wanted to believe that my husband would step up to the plate and take care of things, I knew that wasn't the case.

My mom was released a couple of days later with a concussion and a lot of bruises, but I had to stay a bit longer. They told me that I would need another surgery down the road to take the plate out of my arm and yet another on my injured shoulder. There was no going back to work for me, not for a long while.

At home, unable to use the right side of my body for the next eighteen months and my business in shambles, a friend suggested that I go back to painting to help me heal. I bought a cheap palette of watercolors and a pad of paper, thinking that, at least, watercolors wouldn't make too much of a mess in the house. It never occurred to me that I was worthy of taking up space to heal or making a mess if that's what it took. I was still operating under the old belief that I wasn't worthy of much. I fit myself into a small corner of my bedroom and created a makeshift "studio" to paint in on the floor.

I picked up the brush with my left hand. As a strongly right-side dominant person, I had no control at all. But the paint began to flow, and the images that appeared were nothing like anything I would have expected from a tough bodybuilder like myself—by now, I looked like a warrior, muscled to the hilt and a bit intimidating.

Soft undulating forms and feminine colors graced the pages. I was stunned. Sitting with my paintings, they began to speak to me of something I had long forgotten—myself. I was not just the survivor who had had to armor herself with muscle, but the young girl born to parents who told her that everything about her was wrong and bad. I was the one with ancient memories and inexplicable visions. I began to feel and see myself through those images. Then the writing came. I was scribbling across the pages with words that spoke of my new awareness, like messages from my soul.

And the words began to create a new reality.

As I healed, our business began to fail. I knew I had to create something new out of this mess, or we would lose everything. But even more than that, I knew I needed to create it for myself. There was something pulling at me to grow in a new direction, and it had been showing up in my painting.

My twelve-week transformational program called "Being Physical" debuted while I was still in recovery from the accident. I couldn't train, but I could lead, teach and inspire, and that is exactly what I did. Being in the state I was in physically actually worked in my favor as my clients witnessed me bring myself back. I was unwilling to quit, to accept that I couldn't get strong again. I set the example.

There were twelve participants in that first group, each eager to transform their bodies and their lives. I was on fire as I stood in that room, sharing my journey and coaching them to dig deep and find the courage to do what they believed was impossible for them. They watched me as I did everything I asked them to do, giving them no excuse for quitting. If I could do it in the state I was in, then so could they.

The first program led to another and then another, and the word started spreading as participants emerged transformed. Some left marriages, others started businesses, while most transformed their entire relationship to themselves on all levels. I felt like I had found my calling, and while it was all happening, I was also transforming myself.

After 18 months of recuperation and rehabilitation, I was ready to get my strength back. Each session in the gym, I had to remind myself that the pain of beginning again entailed first experiencing my weakness before I could experience new strength. I had to be willing to be exactly where I was, which was humbling at best. That included both my physical state and the state of my marriage.

I was nearing 50.

I continued to paint even after I recovered. In my late 40s, something new was appearing on my paper—images of pregnant women. The realization hit me that I was ready to give birth to myself and free myself from the abuse. I made a decision, the same one I had made many times before: choosing life over death. I said that if nothing in my marriage changed by my 50th birthday, I would leave. I was going to save my own life and that of my son.

The day arrived. I knew what I had to do. It took another nine months to actually leave, but when I did, it was with only the necessities. I was willing to leave my house, my training equipment and just about everything else behind in order to free myself. Without any idea how I would support my son and myself, I walked out the door.

The next few years were a struggle, but I was happier and healthier than I had been in decades. I met every challenge and grew stronger and more confident. Without someone constantly degrading me, my view of myself began to shift. The words I used to speak about myself and my life took on a new tone, one of self-respect. I was living in a way that my family had said was impossible years ago. I was standing on my own two feet, using my gifts to help others and myself. I was making a difference.

And then the bottom dropped out again. It was a couple of years after the divorce when illness struck again, this time so severely that I had to stop training. I could barely get out of bed. All of the independence I had gained went out the window, and I found myself moving in with the man I was about to marry, dependent upon him for just about everything. I had made another declaration the year before, saying, "I am ready to receive love." Now I felt safe and loved, but my health had hit its lowest point. The loss was devastating. Once again, I questioned whether I had any value.

Years prior, someone had come to my training studio to help me with marketing my business. When he saw my paintings hanging on the walls, he turned to me and said, "You shouldn't be a trainer. You're an artist. That's what you need to do." The loss of everything I thought made me valuable to others opened the door for those words to take flight, and I painted my way through another few years of medical tests and surgeries.

And then came cancer.

It was Christmas 2016. My son and stepdaughter were visiting when I found the lump in my breast. I had always believed that cancer was not my path, so when I felt it, I was in shock. The doctors doubted it was cancer, but months later, when the lump remained, they decided that it was best to take it out. I awoke from surgery, still groggy and out of it. The surgeon was standing over me, and before I had a chance to come to, he said, "You have cancer. We need to talk about chemotherapy." The tears came, and the shock set in. With another surgery two weeks later to remove lymph nodes and then radiation treatment with eleven rods implanted through my breast, I lived in constant fear, traumatized and worn. Any sense of trust in myself was gone.

It was then that I was led to see a past life regression therapist. He told me that my way through this was to follow my heart and do what I love. Simple as that. Somehow, I knew that I was being guided to use my creative abilities in a new way, picking up the thread of something that I loved since childhood. I began my work with fabrics, creating a sacred shawl out of the image on one of my paintings and stringing bead by bead along the edges for thirty-two hours of handwork. It brought me back to myself, a self I had yet to discover fully until I was led to work with a Shaman.

I was in my 60s and knew that something major was going to happen for me before the decade was over, a shift unlike any other. I had had a couple of prophetic readings by psychics and shamans that foretold what was about to occur. Without knowing the details or the timing of any of it, I followed what the illness had guided me to—to create fabrics.

I created obsessively all through the COVID pandemic, so much so that the beginning of arthritis in my hands blossomed into a full-blown inability to work. It mimicked the period when I couldn't train any longer. How was I going to continue my creative work? I knew I couldn't stop. Creating is like breathing to me, somewhat like training was back in the day.

I had been designing fabrics on my computer for the last couple of years, so I knew if I could design fabrics virtually, then I could paint. I was hooked!

Without the arthritis hindering me, I created day and night, literally. The paintings took on a spiritual meaning for me. Messages were coming through, and they seemed to be calling me to share them. I began writing again, this time in the form of an online journal that I shared with others through social media. The response was overwhelming. At the same time, my shamanic practice was deepening, and I found myself on a path that felt both ancient and new. Memories of being a healer, a teacher, a medicine woman, flooded through me, and as an artist, I was tasked with expressing these memories through images.

The paintings evolved over the course of a year or so until a major shift in consciousness occurred through a shamanic ceremony in 2023. I had been gestating a new being, a new life within me, and for the first time, that life had wings. Nine months prior, I had made another declaration of who I was. My words came to life that night as they had so many times before, shifting my reality completely.

I knew that what had begun as a way to heal myself years ago, a return to painting through my non-dominant side, and then to teaching and sharing my experience and wisdom through my program, had now shown me the way back to myself. I had used each illness, each challenge along the way, to expand my awareness and walk closer to the truth of who I am. I had transformed my own life through every word I spoke and every brushstroke I painted. Looking back, it was each declaration of truth, each statement of who I was, that created my next evolution. Though my life began with lies, it blossomed through truth. Our words matter. We hold the power to speak ourselves into being at every moment and create the life of our dreams.

Sheila Certeza Asare

Founder of QUINTESSENCE CREATIONS LLC
Woman-Centered Wellness Coach

https://www.linkedin.com/in/sheilacertezaasare
https://www.facebook.com/sheila.asare.7186
https://thequintessence.life/

Sheila is a passionate coach and co-creator of a wellness practice dedicated to empowering women—especially those navigating Type 2 diabetes and prediabetes—to view their diagnosis as an opportunity to embrace a vibrant, new way of living. With over 30 years of experience in healthcare, she integrates functional medicine coaching, energy code coaching, and SOMA Breath to guide women in reclaiming their health, unlocking their potential, and igniting their inner vitality.

As a woman-centered coach, Sheila provides a supportive, nurturing space where women can rewrite their stories, break free from limiting beliefs, and step fully into their power. She inspires women to ask themselves: Why not me? Why not you? Why not all of us?

Sheila believes it's time to heal, transform, and live the authentic, abundant lives we are meant to lead.

A Spark of Awakening

By Sheila Certeza Asare

"That Day"

It was a typical morning after a long night shift. My body screamed for sleep as I made the 45-minute drive home, the weight of exhaustion pressing on me with every passing minute. "Almost there," I told myself. "A few more minutes, and I'll be in my bed, finally sleeping." No matter how many times I'd driven this route after a grueling 13-hour shift, the exhaustion never got any easier to shake. Sometimes, I'd pull over to the side of the road, desperate for a quick nap, unwilling to risk falling asleep at the wheel. But there was never a moment when I felt completely safe resting there. I hated doing it. That morning, I pushed my weary body to just keep driving, knowing the promise of sleep was waiting for me.

Finally, I was on our street. I remember pulling into the driveway as if it were yesterday, my body aching for rest. But as I stepped out of the car, I saw him—my husband, the father of all three of my children—standing at the door. His expression hit me like a jolt. It wasn't the words he spoke, but the intensity in his face that told me something was wrong. My heart skipped a beat, already sensing the urgency. My mind scrambled, and I heard him say, "Rachel." The word echoed in my head like a siren, a signal that something terrible had happened.

Without thinking, I rushed past him and sprinted toward Rachel's room, my heart pounding in my chest. I knew something was horribly amiss. When I opened the door, I found her—my precious Rachel, the sweet, innocent girl whose laughter filled our home—standing there, changing clothes. Her body was marked by injuries. The sight of her, so brave in the face of pain, tore through me. My heart shattered, but in that instant, all the fatigue, all the exhaustion, disappeared. I couldn't think about sleeping. I couldn't think about anything but getting my children out of there, now.

I gathered my three children—5, 7, and 9 years old—each in a state of confusion, uncertainty, and fear. My body was shaking uncontrollably, my mind spinning in a thousand directions, but I knew I had to act fast. "Hurry!" I urged them, my voice trembling with panic. There was no time to waste. One child couldn't find both shoes, and another was being coaxed by their father to stay in the house. I don't know how we managed it, but somehow, we did. All three children were in the car, and I was behind the wheel.

I drove, my hands shaking on the wheel, my mind racing. We were driving away from our home. The trembling in my body, the knot in my stomach, was all too real. I didn't know exactly what to do next, but there was one thing I was certain of: I had to get my children to safety, and I had to find help for my injured Rachel. Everything else was a blur.

"A Foreign World Began"

Word of our situation reached my family overseas. They came to our side. First, it was my brother, then my parents, each taking turns to be with us and provide the support we so desperately needed. Without my needing to explain anything, help began to pour in. The church stepped in, offering support, and the courthouse connected us to community services. The shame of needing help, accepting help, and the confusion about how to navigate this new lease on life that once held me back faded into the background as we were cared for, loved, and supported by acquaintances who became friends, strangers who became friends, and family who rallied from oceans away. We weren't isolated anymore.

The next two years were defined by constant fear, shame, guilt, and confusion. Fear of my husband's possible revenge—revenge for turning my back on him, on my vows to be there for better or worse, for seeking help from the police and available services. Fear that my children might be deeply emotionally and physically hurt by this new lifestyle.

It was a life of vigilance, where every moment was tinged with the possibility of danger. Our suitcases were always packed—documents, a small stash of food and water, a few changes of clothes, toiletries—everything we might need if we had to run at a moment's notice. This became our reality. Two years of living with a sense of impending danger, never truly feeling safe. Even with the restraining order in place, the protection granted by the court, and the reassurances from the police that our names were in the system and that if we dialed 911, help would arrive without us even needing to say a word, the fear never truly left. These assurances, though comforting, were unfamiliar to me. I was learning to live in a new world—a world where fear was my constant companion.

Weeks turned into months. Months turned into years, and with each passing day, the guilt and shame grew heavier. I had been raised Catholic and had always been a practicing Christian. Divorce was something I learned to view with deep shame and guilt, something that, in my mind, was almost a sin. I was programmed to believe that marriage was for life, that no matter the circumstances, it was a bond that should never be broken.

Despite the fear and the overwhelming sense of danger, I was consumed by the confusion between what my mind and body were telling me was right and the battle against what I had been taught was the "correct" way. Guilt overwhelmed me as I contemplated applying for divorce. Every fiber of my being screamed for freedom, yet I was trapped by the beliefs I had been raised with. The shame of even considering divorce felt like an invisible burden I carried alone.

How could I reconcile my faith with the desperate need to protect my children and myself? How could I balance the beliefs I held so deeply with the painful reality of what we were living through? And how could I lose hope that everything could still change, that our life could get better, that this was just a phase?

Then one day, in the blink of an eye, the divorce was final. I was granted full custody of the children. It felt amazing and liberating—beyond what I had ever expected. This also, officially signaled the beginning of our single-parent household.

"A New Beginning: From Trauma to Survival"

Being a single parent in a place where I had no family nearby was a challenge I never anticipated. Every day felt like a balancing act, constantly juggling between work and home life, with no extended family to turn to for support. I had to become everything for my children: the provider, the caretaker, the emotional anchor. Every decision and every task felt monumental, and there was no one to lean on when it got overwhelming.

Despite the overwhelming circumstances, I knew I needed to give my children opportunities to heal and grow. Each child excelled academically, with teachers recognizing their "gifted abilities." Each child also found joy in soccer, feeling part of something bigger—a community, a family. The soccer family became our second family, a place where we could all experience a sense of belonging. It gave us a space to heal, with each soccer training, match, and cheering moment bringing us closer to a normal life.

Some colleagues at work rallied behind us, allowing me to easily swap shifts so I could participate in my children's school activities. One colleague welcomed me dropping off my three children by 5 a.m. at her house, where she would give them breakfast and take them to school, then pick them up while I worked my 12-13 hour shift. Another teacher at the children's school stayed with them at night when I worked the night shift.

"Learned Behavior, My Programming"

People would often comment on how well I was managing as a single mother, and in many ways, I agreed. I was doing everything I could to ensure there was food on our table, a roof over our heads, and that my children could experience Sunday school and summer church camp. They also developed a deep love for soccer. What started at the YMCA (Young Men's Christian Association) progressed to them being part of the ODP (Olympic Development Program), ECNL (Elite Clubs National League), DA (Development Academy), GAL (Girls Academy League), and MLS (Major League Soccer) Next, each level representing higher training and playing standards. But with that progress came higher costs for travel, equipment, and coaching—adding even more strain on an already tight budget.

It was not just the budget that was stretched thin; my health was being impacted too. The years that followed were marked by the onset of several health conditions. I was diagnosed with diabetes, hypertension, the early stages of kidney failure, and ongoing hypothyroidism. My body was wearing down, and it was becoming harder to keep up with the demands of daily life.

I kept telling myself that one day, this would pass. I had seen so many women in my family sacrifice themselves for their husbands and children. Heck, I even heard these women say, *"You wanted this life, so you should put up with it!"* This was the conditioning I had inherited—messages that reinforced self-sacrifice as the ultimate form of love. These beliefs were woven into my ancestry and mirrored in the lives of the women around me.

So, I soldiered on, believing there was no other choice.

"The Turning Point: Rediscovering Our Power"

But a turning point came when I realized I had fallen deeper into a scarcity mindset—one that my children were witnessing. I knew I needed to snap out of this way of living, not just for myself, but for them as well.

I had to shift from merely surviving to truly living—living with intention and embracing the enjoyment of the present moment.

The process was not easy. Healing didn't come overnight, and the scars—both physical and emotional—ran deep. But I knew that for the children and me to heal, I had to begin with myself.

So, I started carving out small moments for self-care. At first, it felt foreign. *Wasn't this selfish?* But soon, I realized that taking care of myself wasn't just about me. It was about creating a healthier environment for my children and showing them that their mother valued herself. I had to show them that *I mattered*—because I wanted them to know, deep in their hearts, that *they matter*, too. That they are special. That they are loved.

Painfully, but surely, I began to embrace the truth that our time with their father—both the happy moments and the ones we wished had never happened—had brought us to a new version of ourselves. This was life unfolding for our evolution.

This shift in perspective was transformative. It was not just about my healing—it was about giving my children the tools to grow up knowing their worth. I stopped seeing life as an endless series of obstacles or sacrifices for others, as though my time would come later, after everyone else had their needs met. I began to see life as an open field of opportunities, where it was safe for me to be visible and to be cared for. I began to see myself as the creator of my own destiny, no longer defined by past struggles but empowered by the knowledge that I had the power to rewrite my story. I was not broken—nothing needed to be repaired. I am whole. And I was evolving and becoming.

For so long, I believed that I had to prove my worth through sacrifice. Family, church, work, they all told me that love had to be earned. I thought I was not deserving of love unless I worked for it. But in this moment of stillness, I realized that I did not need to earn love. I am love. I was enough as I was. And so were my children.

"Today"

Today, 12 years later, my children are happy, healthy, and thriving. Rachel, who is turning 21 this year, will graduate from Howard University, where she's combining her love for soccer with her studies at her first-choice school. Anna, who is turning 19, will graduate from the University of South Florida in 2026, also from her first-choice university. And Amos, my 17-year-old son, a junior in high school, is aiming to attend university on both academic and sports scholarships—just like his sisters.

These three have been my greatest teachers in this world. They have made motherhood a journey of profound growth and joy. Without them, I would not be the mother I am today, nor the woman that I am today. Their presence helped me not only understand but also embody unconditional love, cherish the purity of innocence, and witness the profound beauty in trust and simply be.

I've found a renewed sense of purpose in co-creating a woman-centered wellness coaching program for women with type 2 diabetes and prediabetes—empowering them to see their diagnoses as invitations to a life of vitality and self-actualization. I find joy in supporting these women break free from their limiting patterns, discovering their own healing tools, and step into their power.

The journey from survival to thriving has transformed my life and my children's. Life is beautiful, though not always easy. We are the architects of our lives, and our healing comes from within. What once seemed like struggles or obstacles are now gifts—opportunities for growth. Pain may feel isolating, but we are never truly alone. We are all connected by the energy that flows through us.

When we shift our mindsets and awaken to who we truly are, we can begin to write our stories from a place of peace and clarity. The choice is ours—it always has been. Every step we take is the perfect one for our journey.

Will you choose, right now, to trust the spark within you and embrace your unfolding awakening?"

Idaliz Romero

Author

https://www.linkedin.com/in/idalizromero
https://www.facebook.com/idaliz.romero
https://www.instagram.com/lizzyret3

Idaliz Romero, a published author born in Puerto Rico and raised in New York, is a compassionate advocate for personal growth, community service, and family. She has devoted her life to uplifting others, beginning her career at a youth shelter, which sparked her passion for nonprofit work.

Over the years, she has impacted lives in various roles, from teaching conversational English to adults to supporting immigration services, finding joy in helping others thrive. A proud mother of two and grandmother to two beautiful girls. She also holds close the memory of her beloved grandson, who, while not physically here, remains with her in spirit.

Now retired in Florida, Idaliz continues to pursue self-development and spiritual growth, embracing each moment to live life to the fullest. With three anthology collaborations, she is now working on her first solo book, set for publication in 2025, hoping to inspire others through her writing.

The Path I Did Not See

By Idaliz Romero

The title of this book, *She Rises, She Leads, She Lives*, caught my attention the moment I read it. How have I risen, led, and lived my life? Then, I started recalling the experiences I have had in my life that express these words.

She Rises:

I have risen from a childhood filled with sadness. Abandoned by my parents and lived with relatives where I felt unwanted and unloved. I lived a lonely life as a child, even though I had siblings. The experiences that we shared together actually made a rift between us that made it impossible for us to be close the way siblings should be. The rift is there, but now that we are older, we are working on getting close. I have already lost two siblings without having the opportunity to bridge that rift between us.

As for feeling wanted and loved, I was blessed to have married a loving husband who made me feel so loved, even in times of disagreement. I knew without a doubt of his love until his passing. Which left a hole in my life. I was also given the gift of two amazing children who remind me every day that they love me and are proud of me. We have a relationship that I never thought existed. My upbringing and the relationships that surrounded me as a child and teenager gave me a different view of what I thought family relationships were. I never felt or knew what love felt like until I married and had my children. That feeling was something I thought was only on television, but it was not real.

After learning about loving relationships, I started to share it with my extended family. I was the first one to say "I love you" to my family every time we said goodbye in person or on the phone, and I still do. I still remember the expression on my aunt's face the first time I said it. Those words were not said in my family ever. I had to learn how to love, and that love has created the family that I dreamed about. A loving husband and the love of my children. Now, feeling the love of my granddaughters, who are excited to see me and plead with me to extend my visit with them, brings joy to my life. Learning to accept and love myself is my highest rise. Understanding that being loved by others is a blessing but loving myself is the greatest gift I can give myself. When I love myself, it gives others permission to love me as well.

She Leads:

As a young girl, I was not a leader, or I thought I was not. But what do you call a person who has achieved so many firsts in her family? See, I was always the first person to take that step that no one was willing to take, to take chances, and to experience new things. What do I mean? Keep reading, and you will understand.

I was the first to speak up as a young girl in my family when I did not agree with what was said or done, which, of course, came with some negative consequences that were meant to deter me from doing it again. Of course, that did not happen. Growing up in a household where abuse was a norm, I did not realize that there was another way to live. Becoming a mother gave me a new perspective, which led me to be the first to break the cycle of abuse that the generations before had lived with, including myself and my siblings. It was a difficult cycle to break as I had no other models to follow, but I knew that that was not the kind of life I wanted for my children, knowing the lasting effects that it had on me. It was the most difficult to learn a new way of living for me because physical, mental, and verbal abuse was prevalent throughout my childhood and teen years. But I felt deeply that there had to be a better way to, and I made the choice to change the legacy for my children and future generations.

Basic education was a requirement, but graduating from high school was not a priority for others in my family. It was for me. I love learning; reading was my obsession. Maybe because it took me to places far from my own reality. I became the first one to graduate. I wanted to continue learning, not necessarily because I liked school, but because I had a thirst for knowledge. By graduating from high school, I made a path for the younger generation in my family to follow. I was also the first to attend college.

In many families from my generation, children did not leave home, especially women, until they were married. I broke the norm. At the age of 19, I left my home and moved into my first apartment. I worked days and attended college at night, which did not leave much time for anything else, but I loved my new freedom and responsibilities. Was it easy? Definitely not, but it was worth it to have the freedom to make my own choices, my own experiences, and my own mistakes. If you asked me, would I do it again? My reply would be a resounding yes.

My younger years were spent in Brooklyn, New York, where I lived since the age of 8. That community was all that my family and I knew. No one ventured out. They lived there, married there, and raised children there as well. I felt there was more, but I did the same: I married and had children there. Until an opportunity to venture out showed up. I did not take a moment to think about it. I wanted to see if there was something better for my family and myself. I became the first in my family to leave Brooklyn and move out into a new adventure. After that first move, it became much easier to make the next move. I have lived in Philadelphia, New Jersey, Utah, and Florida. I am not sure where my life will take me next, but I enjoy living in different communities and meeting new people. As for my family, you guessed it, they are still in Brooklyn. As a joke, I am referred to as the "gypsy" in the family. Did all the moving I made go well, no, but the lessons I learned from each one have given me the knowledge for whatever move I am making next.

I was also the first to elope. Our families were against our marriage because he was younger than me, but that did not matter to us. Without their support, we decided to just elope after dating for six months. Of course, it was not something that was approved of, but we knew that this was what we wanted to do. Many comments were made, including the prediction that our marriage would last two years. But with our love and determination, we had a marriage that lasted twenty-three years. Was it perfect, no, but we were committed to our relationship and our children.

To me, a leader is a person who has done something extraordinary, for example, an athlete, a celebrity, or a famous writer. I learned not so long ago that anyone can lead, as long as they are willing to take chances, move out of their comfort zone, or take that first step.

Oh, I am also the first writer in my family. I have collaborated on three anthology books. Writing has always been easy for me as I have been writing journals my entire life. But writing a book is so different and rewarding. It is funny that I am the only one who enjoys reading and writing. It makes it a little difficult to feel like I belong or that I am part of my extended family. I feel that I was placed with them to make a difference. To show them the possibilities that are around them.

Entering the world of network marketing is something that I had to learn on my own, as no one in my family has been involved in it. Which I want to share with them. I want to show them there is a new and different way to live a better life.

There are so many things that I have experienced first, and I truly hope that all that they have seen me achieve or accomplish may someday open the door for them to all that is possible for their lives and that they may share my legacy with future generations.

She Lives:

I have lived, and I am still living an incredible life. If I was asked a couple of years ago what I thought of my life, incredible would not have been the word I used. A couple of years ago, I would have said that I had an unhappy life. With all that I had lived as a child, a teenager, and even as an adult, I was filled with anger, resentment, pain, and much more.

Then, I made a commitment to myself that my past experiences and heartache would not be part of my present or future. I dedicated my time to learning about myself. Who I really was, not what I was told, or what I lived, but the real me.

It took facing the pain that I had inside and how damaged I thought I was to understand. But not just that, I had to learn to forgive myself and others. That acknowledgment laid the foundation for my new life. The road has not been easy, and there was a time when I said to myself, "What is the point?" Now I understand. In order to live the incredible life, I have now, I had to take inventory of all that I was holding inside. The memories of being unloved, unwanted, and abused. The pain of feeling lonely from childhood to adulthood. Knowing inside me that there had to be more. That this could not be the life that I was meant to live. Struggling to find a place where I belong, which I found with my husband and children.

I had to reinvent myself more than once in order to truly know who I was and what I wanted for my life. After experiencing losses, I started to search inside me by sitting quietly by myself and giving my inner child a voice. The more I sat quietly and focused on seeing her and letting her know that she was loved and that she was wanted, I started changing. I held her close, letting her know that she was not alone and that I would protect her. That started the healing process.

I started focusing on forgiveness. How can I forgive those who hurt me? It was a very difficult task, but if I wanted to change, I had to go all the way. I began to learn to love myself. The way that I felt about my children helped me to understand how to love myself. Now that I understand love, how can I feel the same way about myself? I wanted to live a life without the pain of the past. I am grateful that I made the choice to forgive. Forgiveness can open your heart to understanding and that made all the difference in my life.

My life took a different path from the one I thought I was going to, and along the way, I have encountered many challenges, but I have also encountered friendships, kindness, support, and encouragement. Now, I live a life filled with love from my children and granddaughters. Whenever I look at them, I am reminded of my past and what I would have lost if I had not taken the time to love and forgive. The joy I feel now blurs the pain of the past and all that I have survived.

Conclusion:

I hope that you, the reader, may rise from whatever challenges you are facing or faced in your life. Remember that you are not alone. The phoenix rises from the ashes, and so can you!

Leaders many times do not see themselves as leaders, but your experiences, your challenges, and your story can be what someone else may need to hear to lead them to change and discover who they are.

Learn to live your life to the fullest. Challenges or heartaches may come, and no one is exempt from them, but what you do with those experiences can destroy you or become the lessons you need to grow stronger and live the life you deserve.

My desire is that my story and my experiences have given you a small glimmer of hope that even when you think it is too dark to see a brighter future, you will see the tiniest light leading you to a better path.

Kathy George, MS, CMHC

Reclaiming Hope Coach
Trauma-Competent Care for Grief Transformation

https://www.linkedin.com/in/kathy-george-coach
https://www.facebook.com/ReclaimingHopeCoach
https://www.instagram.com/reclaiminghopecoach/
https://linktr.ee/kathyreclaiminghope
https://reclaiminghopecoach.com/
https://hope.reclaiminghopecoach.com/hope

Kathy George, MS, CMHC, is the Founder and Trauma-Competent Grief Coach at Reclaiming Hope Coach. Her journey into grief work began with the profound loss of her son, Trevor, to Sudden Unexplained Death in Childhood (SUDC), followed by her own battle with breast cancer. These experiences deepened her understanding of grief and trauma's impact, inspiring her to pursue a Master's in Clinical Mental Health Counseling.

Certified in grief education, hypnosis, and as a Quantum Alignment System Practitioner, Kathy integrates clinical expertise with holistic approaches, including Advanced StoryLab facilitation and various healing modalities, to support clients through their healing journey. Her HOPE Healing Journey framework guides individuals from grief to growth, helping them honor their present, overcome their past, partner with possibility, and empower their potential.

Based in Tennessee, Kathy provides virtual coaching worldwide, creating safe spaces where clients can transform their pain into resilience while rediscovering hope and purpose.

Standing on My Story:
Transforming Grief into Purpose

By Kathy George, MS, CMHC

The Old Me

Ahhh, when I think back to the old me (big smile), I was so sure of so many things. I loved and lived by the law of attraction. The world, to me, was a mirror of my thoughts and energy. I believed in the beauty of life, the strength of love, and the power of our minds to shape reality. I was a mother, a wife, and a dreamer—someone who saw every day as a canvas of possibility.

I practiced intentional positivity, trusting that good energy attracted good outcomes. The law of attraction wasn't just an idea; it was a lifestyle, a way of aligning my heart and mind with the limitless possibilities I believed the universe held for me. I visualized my dreams, spoke them into existence, and approached life with joyful expectancy. I understood that the energy of our emotions created a frequency and that we attracted experiences aligned with that frequency. Positive emotions equaled positive frequency, which led to positive experiences. Negative emotions... well, you get the idea. Besides, spending most of my time in a good mood felt like a great way to live. I had life figured out—or so I thought.

At night, I would fall asleep exhausted—from hard work, parenting, and the responsibilities of running a household—but my heart was full of gratitude. I felt lucky to have so much in my life to tire me out! Life was beautiful, messy, and perfectly mine. I was certain I had discovered the formula for happiness and fulfillment, and I trusted that the universe and I were working hand in hand to keep it that way.

When It All Fell Apart

But if we truly create our reality, how could I have created this?

The sudden and unexplained death of my beloved son, Trevor, at age six. My husband's terrifying health crisis with open-heart surgery. A triple-negative breast cancer diagnosis during a pandemic for me. And, as if to drive the point home, partial facial paralysis that followed treatment. Each event chipped away at the foundation of who I thought I was. The life I had built with love, intention, and hope felt shattered.

It's no surprise that after all this, I felt cracked and fragile. I moved through each day, surviving but not truly living, caught in a pattern of blame and endless "Why me?" questions. I was adrift, feeling that life had happened to me, without agency or direction. My once-loving relationship with the law of attraction had turned into a love-hate, WTF relationship. How could I reconcile the belief that we attract our experiences with these unthinkable losses? How had the principles I once held so dear seemingly abandoned me when I needed them most?

The Weight of Loss

Grief and loss became unyielding companions, ever-present even in small moments of joy. I still sought out those moments, but it took time to learn how to feel both joy and grief (or any two opposing emotions) at once. Parenting my living children became bittersweet—a constant reminder that one child was gone. I couldn't parent Trevor as I could them, so I vowed to be the best parent possible to them. Fierce mama bear has NOTHING on grieving, fiercer mama bear.

As grief does, I would find myself overcome with emotion, missing Trevor. I allowed what I called "grief bursts," moments when I could cry freely before forcing myself to "be positive." I'd retreat into isolation until I felt I could fake it enough to rejoin the world. Friends and family didn't understand, and I realized they couldn't unless they had experienced the unimaginable loss of a child. And no one wishes that on anyone.

Well-intentioned but misguided people told me to "move on," but to any bereaved parent, this phrase is an insult. Would you ever "move on" from loving or caring about your children? I didn't think so.

Outwardly, I kept going forward, but inside, I was adrift—surviving, not living. I didn't realize then how much the stories I told myself—about blame, helplessness, and despair—kept me stuck. I was trapped in a narrative of powerlessness.

The Breaking Point

At some point, after Trevor died, I found myself grappling with the profound changes in my brain and body. Trauma had hijacked my ability to see possibilities, locking me into survival mode. The simplest vision of a different future—let alone pursuing it—felt almost impossible. I began reading about the impact of trauma on the nervous system and how it dysregulates our ability to function. It helped me understand why I felt so stuck.

In 2018, after a 21-year career in wireless, I was laid off. Instead of fear, I felt relief—YAHOO! Finally, I had the opportunity to pursue what I had been yearning for: a chance to go back to school and study grief, loss, and trauma. My plan was simple but profound: to become the person I had needed after Trevor's death. Grief services were hard to find, and professionals who hadn't experienced the loss of a child often admitted they couldn't fully grasp the depth of that pain.

I've often wondered if the unprocessed trauma of those years played a role in my breast cancer diagnosis. I still wonder. When I received that diagnosis, it felt like a wake-up call. Staring down mortality, I knew I couldn't wait for "time to heal all wounds." Life had already shown me that time alone was no healer—Trevor's death had proven that. So, I began asking myself different questions: *If this is how life might end, how do I want to live it? What do I want my days to look like?*

This shift in perspective didn't come all at once. It arrived in whispers—small moments of clarity amidst the chaos. Significant changes followed, including an out-of-state move that symbolized a fresh chapter. For the first time in a long time, I began to ask myself: *Am I at cause, or am I at effect? And where do I want to be? What I knew was that I wanted to be at cause.* That single shift sparked something I hadn't felt in years: agency.

The Neuroscience of Change

As I pursued a master's degree in mental health, certifications in grief, and training in trauma reprocessing and energy medicine, I began to understand why I had been stuck for so long. Trauma had physically changed my brain.

Grief often lodges itself in the areas of the brain responsible for processing present-time events. This causes the past to feel immediate and unending. However, as I learned more about the brain's ability to change, I found a glimmer of hope. Neuroplasticity—the brain's ability to rewire itself—showed me that healing was possible. I also discovered liminal cells, specialized neurons that activate when we envision new possibilities. This discovery felt like a lifeline: I could move from survival mode to a place of creation.

As I began reprocessing my traumas, I noticed profound changes. With my nervous system regulated, I could see possibilities that had once been obscured. When I missed Trevor, I no longer only felt the emptiness of his absence. I began to see signs of him—moments that felt like gifts rather than wounds. These subtle shifts transformed my grief, allowing me to heal. This type of healing is something I can't recommend enough to anyone navigating grief.

Finding Emotional Balance

Even as I made progress, reminders of my challenges still surfaced daily. The energy of grief, pain, and trauma still felt heavy. But I made a conscious decision to integrate the lessons I'd learned and release their emotional hold on my life. I began asking myself new questions, ones that shifted my focus from *Why me?* to *What now?*:

- How can I honor Trevor's life in ways that reach beyond his years?
- What purpose can I find in this chapter of my life?
- How do I begin to create meaning from all this pain?

With these lessons intact and my emotions expressed, I turned my attention to raising my vibration. I sought out the small joys that lifted me emotionally: feeling the sun on my face, watching the birds, listening to live music, and witnessing my kids grow into their unique selves. These moments became my anchors, pulling me upward on the emotional scale. For the first time in years, I thought, *Maybe I'm on my way.*

Keep Turning Over Stones: Starting with Grace and Compassion

Then came the facial paralysis. I stopped everything. In a sense, I gave up—or maybe I surrendered. I joked that this ailment was "better" than cancer, but in reality, it crippled me. I couldn't even pretend to smile. The idea of "fake it till you make it" was out the window; forced positivity was impossible.

I remember the day I hit my breaking point. I threw my hands up and thought, *Okay, UNCLE! What the *&?^% am I supposed to do now?* And then, almost like a whisper, I heard: *Pause. Grace. See the pattern.* With that, I vowed to stop trying so hard. I had no idea what to do anyway. I needed to fall back into life and let it unfold.

This was excruciatingly difficult for me. My knowledge of the law of attraction told me that until I could get ahead of the energy, life would feel like it was being pulled backward. I reflected on my life and thought, *I know I lived through it, but it feels so heavy.* Pretending none of it had happened wasn't an option. I accepted every loss and integrated every lesson, but the weight still felt like standing in sludge.

MY STORY! I began asking myself: *How can I stand on my story instead of in it?* That single thought became a turning point.

A New Framework: Standing on My Story

When I was searching for a way forward, I discovered Karen Curry Parker's Quantum Alignment System (QAS), a comprehensive framework integrating Quantum Human Design (QHD) (https://quantumhumandesign.com) with evidence-based tools for transformation. This approach combines the wisdom of QHD with narrative reframing to create lasting change. Within QAS, I found a method that deeply resonated with me: StoryLab.

StoryLab process, as developed by Karen Curry Parker, offered a way to explore and transform the personal narratives I had carried for years—the stories of loss, blame, and helplessness that kept me stuck. This process wasn't about erasing the past but about intentionally rewriting my story, giving it new meaning, and empowering me to move forward. Using my Quantum Human Design Chart as a tool, I uncovered areas where old patterns were holding me back. StoryLab then guided me to transform these insights into an empowered narrative.

There might be a different pattern—a better pattern—available. StoryLab offers a transformative approach to rewriting your narrative, guiding you beyond the conditioned stories and beliefs that have kept you stuck. This profound process reveals a narrative rooted in alignment, abundance, and fulfillment. What makes StoryLab so distinctive is its use of your Quantum Human Design Chart as a tool to help you see your experiences through a fresh, empowered lens.

By working with your Quantum Human Design Chart, you can uncover your life purpose and soul curriculum, transforming your chart into a powerful storytelling framework. As Karen Curry Parker says, *When you tell a better story, you live a better life.*

What makes the Quantum Life Purpose Process and StoryLab so extraordinary is its deeply personalized nature, uniquely tailored to you. The process draws from the high expression of the gates in your Quantum Human Design Chart, organizing them into a clear and empowering narrative. This allows you to step out of the conditioned stories and limiting themes that reside in your mind and into a new, authentic narrative that aligns with your highest potential, no matter what you have experienced.

Conditioning, Lovability, and Self-Worth

Conditioning is the result of repeated thoughts, beliefs, and experiences that shape the stories we tell ourselves. Over time, these stories become themes in our lives—familiar patterns that dictate how we perceive and respond to the world. They often operate subconsciously, keeping us tethered to old, unproductive narratives.

One of the most damaging effects of conditioning is how it erodes our sense of lovability and self-worth. Loss, pain, and failure can make us question our inherent value, convincing us that we are unworthy of love, care, or support. These conditioned beliefs can trap us in cycles of doubt and self-criticism, making it difficult to see the truth: that our worth is not tied to our circumstances, but to the essence of who we are.

The beauty of the new story created through StoryLab is its power to decondition these ingrained patterns. By crafting a new narrative, you open the door to an alternative view of your life, one that reflects the highest expression of who you are. This new perspective acts as a catalyst for your reticular activating system (RAS) to shift focus. Before, the conditioned stories I told myself only allowed me to see what I knew: the pain, the loss, the limitation. The RAS kept me stuck in these patterns, filtering my reality through this narrow lens. But as I rewrote my story, the RAS began to filter in the new possibilities—ones that I hadn't allowed myself to see before. The more I reread my story, the more my brain's filters began to focus on hope, possibility, and fresh directions. As my RAS continues to filter in elements from this new narrative, it helps bring those possibilities into my awareness, reshaping my perceptions, decisions, and ultimately, my reality. It's like adjusting a lens on a camera—changing what the lens picks up and how it focuses on what's truly possible.

Deconditioning is a journey—a process of unraveling the influences of societal, familial, and cultural narratives that no longer serve you. It's not an overnight change, but one that requires dedicated work at the subconscious level. As someone trained in hypnosis, I understand that real transformation often starts beneath the surface, where old patterns and limiting beliefs are stored—where we can uncover and release the beliefs and stories that have kept you stuck. Recognizing the potential for change and the possibilities that await is step one!

Through StoryLab, you're not just rewriting a story; you're reclaiming your lovability and self-worth. It's about rediscovering that you are inherently worthy of love, belonging, and abundance, regardless of what you've endured. As you work through this, you begin to rewrite the narrative, aligning it with your highest potential and reconnecting to the truth of who you are.

My StoryLab Journey: From Grief to Empowerment

In my own journey, the transformative power of rewriting my narrative became a reality through my personal StoryLab process. It wasn't just a method—it was a profound and deeply personal exploration of the stories I carried and the ones I longed to create. This process allowed me to move beyond the conditioned patterns and beliefs that had kept me stuck, opening a path to alignment, abundance, and fulfillment.

What follows is the story that emerged from this journey. It reflects how I used StoryLab to shift from grief to growth, from limitation to love, and from pain to purpose. May it serve as both a testament to the power of this work and an invitation to consider what rewriting your own narrative could mean for your life.

This is my new story, thoughtfully crafted with the gate names preserved in alignment with my Quantum Human Design.

I, Kathy, powerfully and passionately declare that my Life Purpose is to embrace the emotional depth and transformative power of new experiences (Gate 36: Exploration) and share inspired visions that guide others toward hope and possibility (Gate 11: The Conceptualist). To do this, I allow, create, and receive the gift of emotional balance and harmony, even in times of intense challenge (Gate 6: Impact) and the courage to express my authentic voice with clarity and grace, knowing that the right timing always supports my truth (Gate 12: The Channel) as part of the foundation of the deep well of creativity that I AM.

My Heart and Soul are driven by a focused and determined energy that reminds me to channel my efforts into what truly matters (Gate 9: Convergence) and a commitment to realign and improve patterns in my life, healing the brokenness and bringing a sense of purpose to the pain (Gate 18: Re-alignment). I know that nurturing this drive gives me the energy and passion to continue to align myself with my Purpose. I embrace this challenge as part of my learning and growth process. I know that when I encounter an inner conflict, this is a symptom of my own expansion and indicates that I am learning and growing. I'm always doing it "right." I'm always growing and changing.

My personal learning energy teaches me the courage to express transformative communication and grace (Gate 12: The Channel) by empowering me to speak my truth, even when it feels risky. This gate encourages me to trust in divine timing, allowing my voice to reach others with clarity and impact. I also embrace the wisdom of compassion and adaptability (Gate 15: Compassion), helping me find unity amidst diversity and teaching me the importance of balancing extremes in my environment and relationships. When I master these inner lessons, I am blessed by faith and trust in abundance (Gate 55: Faith), which gives me the confidence to embrace life's flow, even during uncertain times. I am also gifted with the ability to form deep attunement and connection with others (Gate 19: Attunement), creating bonds that reflect mutual care and understanding, even in challenging circumstances.

My Spiritual Purpose and Path are to stay grounded in focus and clarity, even when life feels overwhelming, trusting that every step aligns me with my greater calling (Gate 9: Convergence) and to use my wisdom to recalibrate and bring about healing, transforming challenges into opportunities for growth and evolution (Gate 9: Convergence). I call on these energies when I am in need of greater alignment with my Purpose. I know that I need to master the courage to face the unexpected and emerge stronger from life's disruptions, sharing my resilience with the world (Gate 51: Initiation) and the bravery to embrace my spiritual awakening through life's trials, using them to guide others toward healing (Gate 51: Initiation) to deepen what I am here to share with the world. I use this knowledge and wisdom to communicate through a fiery passion that ignites hearts and inspires change (Gate 30: Passion) and a trust in the steady rhythm of life's cycles, knowing that every phase holds purpose (Gate 5: Consistency).

I share the full expression of who I am with the world through these energies. I play a unique role in the evolution of Humanity, and I have a vital and irreplaceable place in Divine Order. I honor all of who I am, and I deeply and completely love and accept myself.

Living the New Story

Today, I see a future not defined by loss but shaped by the resilience, compassion, and hope I've cultivated. Healing isn't about "moving on"; it's about holding love and grief in the same space, allowing them to weave together into a richer, more authentic life. The pain doesn't control me anymore—it's part of my story, adding texture and depth, but it's not the whole picture.

As a grief coach and Quantum Alignment System Practitioner, I understand that healing doesn't happen in isolation. It's a journey that asks us to rewrite the narratives we carry. I've seen it firsthand: it's possible to reclaim your life from even the darkest places.

If you're feeling buried by your grief, ask yourself:

- What would it mean to stand on your story, instead of being trapped by it?
- What light can you bring forth from the darkness?
- How can you start writing a new chapter, even one sentence at a time?

Your story doesn't end with grief. It begins with how you choose to rise and what you create from this moment.

Call to Action

This is my story—not one of loss, but of resilience and transformation. It's about finding light in the darkest places and guiding others toward healing. But it's not just my story—it's yours too.

If your story is holding you back, it's time to rewrite your narrative. Take the first step today:

- What story are you telling yourself?
- How is it shaping your life?

Reach out for support and begin reframing your journey. Let's explore how you can turn your pain into purpose.

Together, we can rewrite your story. You are not alone.

If you're in profound grief right now, know I'm holding space for you. Allow yourself to feel what needs to be felt—it's okay to let the waves come. When you're ready, reflect on your current narrative. Is it serving you? If not, consider this your invitation to start rewriting it.

You are here for a reason, and the world needs you—just as you are. If I can rise, so can you. Your story, with all its challenges, matters. Stand on it, learn from it, and know that someone, somewhere, will be inspired by you.

Trevor's legacy lives on—not only through me but in every life I've had the privilege to touch. His life has become a beacon of love, guiding me and others toward healing and connection.

Step into your intention and embrace your power to create change. You are at cause in your life, and you have the ability to transform your pain into purpose, one brave step at a time. Your story matters, and its power to heal—both yourself and others—cannot be underestimated.

Tara Swanson

Body Mind Ignite & StretchLab
Fitness & Nutrition Consultant

http://linkedin.com/in/tara-swanson-015295192
https://www.facebook.com/taraleannhenderson?mibextid=LQQJ4d
https://www.instagram.com/taraswanson/
https://www.threads.net/@taraswanson

Tara Swanson is a speaker, writer, educator and public health professional who pairs her passion for lifelong learning and growth (as a survivor in multiple arenas) with her desire to activate the no-fear attitude in others to confidently step into their authentic self so they may live out their intended purpose. Tara is a self-proclaimed late bloomer and idealist (sometimes to a fault). She believes we all have a Superhero waiting to shine. Tara received her BSED, MED, and MPH from the University of Missouri-Columbia. Over the past decade she has written successful grants for organizations in the U.S., 85% of her college prep students have been admitted to Ivy League and UC schools, and while teaching writing and speaking on campus about domestic abuse and trauma at Missouri Valley College students were motivated to start a domestic/sexual abuse organization. Her programs Fast Track to Success for teens and Body-Mind Ignite for individuals and businesses each uniquely prepare clients to realize their Stellar Success.

Crash and Bounce - But Whatever You Do, Don't Let Them Put You On Their Train

By Tara Swanson

ANXIETY

Though she appeared confident on the outside, inside she struggled with self-doubt and the pressure of societal expectations.

Changemaker Changemaker what is your thing?
Not biting bullets, just dice it and splice it.
Sugar and salt,
Shake it up solid.
Foundational Loco - No time to choko
Lois Lane feeling no pain.
Peter Pan , Tinker Bell staking their claim.
Bonnie and Clyde down for the ride.
Stare in my eyes -
Tell me Changemaker, what's your demise ?

2024

Beating the traffic to get to the quiet beach before work, singing-along to, "It's in the Way That You Use It", by Eric Clapton, after 52 years, I fully embrace the "me" I have become and was created to be. As usual, I'm ready to get my fix of the ocean before I start my workday. Touching, feeling, smelling, and hearing the waves brings me to life each day. I'm Still hanging on every word of the conversation I had with my middle son on the phone yesterday. I look one more time at the pictures of my youngest son from two days ago when I spent the afternoon with him. I try one more time to digest the text I received two days ago from my oldest son, which stated he is limiting his contact with me. In this moment I felt like heaven and hell are embracing me and smothering me all at once. I prayed I would not cross anyone's path as I crossed the street to get to my morning workout. My face was contorted in the most confused sort of way- joy, pain, rot, rebirth.

* * * *

When we make a conscious decision to choose the pieces of self that we want to enhance and take into the future, we are then able to transform and showcase our Superhero capabilities moving forward. Lesson - The Grace and Grit Imperative

1975

Three years old, during the children's sermon at church, was the first time I met ANXIETY. I now know she is the biggest bully I've ever encountered. She has taunted me for 49 years. She has motivated me to dig holes in my shoes, throw up in silence and pray people don't notice when I walked into a room. As I followed the leader of the line, with the other three year olds, to the front of the sanctuary for the children's sermon, I smiled as "Little Miss Freedom". Pastor Maas told us a story that was kid friendly and made us smile. Then it was time for each of us to give an answer to the question he posed. I don't even remember what the question was and I don't remember what my answer was but what I do vividly recall is that when I gave my answer the church went silent. I mean crickets. It felt like the silence lasted forever. I knew that my answer must have been unique, and there must be something wrong with me. Why didn't I just sit in silence and pretend to be clueless? Shaking, while walking back to my seat to find my parents, ANXIETY had defeated me and would to take over and control me and for the next decade of my life. For the next several years of my life, I became "Princess Timid".

1980-1986

"You are Dr. Swanson, the Superintendent's daughter",

Walking into science class and ducking into my front row seat I heard the burley, unkempt science teacher belt out," I think I'll give you the worst textbook here so your dad gets to see how badly the science department needs more money." I could feel the heat from inside firing up my face, turning it 10 shades of red. My toes immediately clinched up and started digging holes in my brand new shoes. That bitch ANXIETY was here again!

Then there were the expectations I put on myself. Girls were supposed to want to be cheerleaders and models.

Yes, I will be cheerleader. I need to be skinnier... The laxative trick.

* * * *

1987- 1994

I was home. I knew I fit in. I welcomed the move to San Diego. I finally felt a sense of belonging. It was the most appropriate fit. I stood out and at the same time belonged just like a fish in water. I was so comfortable - not singled out for being shy or pretty, for good or bad. I felt free to be me.

"T -Watch me on my first wave and then I'm gonna come back and set you up on the longboard that we waxed last night." Getting up on that first wave was incredible! I felt so good, I pushed that bully ANXIET right off of my board! FREEDOM came out of hiding ... It was so awesome to see her again and to feel her presence.

"That was totally RAD!" Authenticity, and excitement - back to the Freedom I used to be.

Even though she was typically now in hiding, ANXIETY would peek here head around once in awhile just to make sure she was keeping me on my toes.

Yes I will model but I need to be skinnier- I want to be a runway model, not a fitness model... The laxative trick. Fitness models are just not what I thought I should aspire to be but that's where I was placed in L.A. Don't eat, take more laxatives. Am I getting closer?

* * * *

It's been a slow unwinding to get back to writing poetry while working out and being led back to the processes that work best for me. Getting onto the wrong trains, hiding from ANXIETY, trying to be like everyone and being thrown into the fire have led me to a new

kind of light. I've been charging uphill through the deep, sticky, muck for 15 years... two steps forward before the next slide back. What is this life? What is my purpose And how will I ever redeem myself in my boys' eyes? Did I make a mistake? Would it have been better to stay in the shadow of "his" rules? Endless lists of rights and wrongs that changed at his discretion? Maybe it would've been better (I used to wonder) to follow his mother's path. Become complacent and sit in a life of oppression and degradation? Allow myself to be a pawn for a man who had big fears, a man who would rather use his wife as a decoy and watch her be eaten away by disease and self loathing?

This is the journey into the abyss I slid into and thought I would never return from, only to find a new and very real freedom, a true knowing of the harsh realities of the world we live in, the realities that many people choose to close their eyes to. So many would rather hop on the status quo train and be a rule follower than to build their own train. But many like me, crash, get thrown into the fire, get to be forged by the fire and are allowed to bounce to the next lesson. An unequivocal potential of greatness, love and freedom cannot be inherited, learned in books, or even earned by a self prescribed list of rights and wrongs. True knowing can only be experienced when you are willing to say yes to your truth path.

I tried so hard to take their path, the one most traveled, but was unsuccessful every time. That path gave me shin splints, made me bleed, made me ache and cringe in disbelief, and filled me with ANXIETY.

1972 - 1975 I refer to myself as "Freedom". My lineage is comprised of strong women and loyal men. I've been told that on January 9, 1972. I entered this world with heart shaped nostrils. The real love that comes from deep within, wanting to be accepted and wanting to love unconditionally has taken me down many times. My parents know how to work hard and work together. They love unconditionally. My brother was born four years after I came into the world and we were a happy family of four. Don't get me wrong - No Family is perfect. All families have struggles. I was very sheltered.

* * * *

It's been a very long, dark road.

How do I ever make it up to my sons who have become the highest caliber young men? How do I prove to them that they are the loves of my life and I would die for them in any moment. With every breath I take, I hurt for their sacrifice of giving up a peaceful childhood. I made sure everything was perfect for them. Even before they were born I refused to take a sip of caffeine and only ate the healthiest foods. I played Baby Mozart in the car to make sure they were being stimulated while in the womb. After they were born I only fed them organic food, didn't dare give them plastic bottles, was the first mom to sign her name on the roomparent list for all three of classes throughout their younger years. Damn I wish they could remember these things!

* * * *

1994-

At the end of my undergrad teetering between wanting to go to club med, and knowing I needed to finish my degree and get a job, a grown-up job, a real job, I somehow found myself back in the Midwest.

* * * *

1996

Today I was going to meet my fiance's parents. We would be stopping there on the way to one of my fiance's friend's weddings. I had respectfully and thoughtfully gone through at least six outfits because I was informed it would be in my best interest to dress down

from what the typical KC or San Diego girl would wear to a wedding. I settled on the moss green and off-white tweed fall short dress with a matching crop jacket. At the last minute I exchanged my heels for some tall tan boots just to make sure I was not too

dressed up. We pulled into his parents' drive, after passing through the only stoplight in town, so he could grab something on the way to the wedding. From across the two lane highway I heard a gruff voice bellow, "that must be the city priss you were talking about".

I felt ANXIETY coming out, ready to bully. I heard her snicker, "see, you don't fit in here." I did not turn around to see who owned the voice. I just looked forward Frantically whispering to ANXIETY, "just go away and be quiet. I'm ignoring you." I looked to my fiancé, hoping he would tell the guy to be quiet. Instead, he just laughed.

We continue to walk behind the house onto the open land until we rounded the corner of a fence line. Just as we rounded the corner, I felt a thumb on my boot. I looked down to see blood splattered everywhere.

"Ah, ain't nothing that a little pig testicle is gonna hurt." Snickers echoed off the land. This is how I was introduced to my soon to be father-in-law.

* * * *

Later down the line I would see how terribly my mother-in-law was treated when there was a teenage boy allowed to live in her house. That crazy-ass 16 year old pulled down my mother-in-law Schorts while she was wobbling at the stove trying to cook for everyone. Multiple Sclerosis had been gnawing away at her body since she was in her 20s. By this time she was nearly wheelchair bound. The whole family sat around and laughed when he did this. I've never had a problem standing up for other people, and until this point, I really had never had to stand up for myself. After dinner I took the boys downstairs and that ignorant kid followed. He started to taunt me. I turned around and pinned that little shit down on the floor. I was so angry. I advised him never to harass my sons' grandma again - that was the last time that kid dared to be in a room with me. In retrospect, I might feel a tad bit bad that the poor kid had no idea that even though my outside looked like a city priss I knew how not to be one. Between my mom' and dad's sides of the family, I had a sturdy physique and intuitively knew how to finesse in a scrappy manner when necessary. For the next 10 years, I researched MS in an attempt to help my mother-in-law get access to new info on MS coming out of the University. There was an unspoken respect between myself and my mother in law. Before having my three boys I had two miscarriages, and she immediately reached out to get the best doctor to see me. I am forever grateful for her help. She passed away a couple of years ago.

* * * *

1999- My first son was born a week before his due date, eager to face the world from this day forward. He was the most beautiful site I had ever seen. He looked at me with his full head of platinum blonde hair and bright blue eyes, "Hey Mom". From the second he entered the world, I saw that he would be a confident leader with solid integrity.

2001 my second amazing son entered the world on his due date, with his mesmerizing, deep, wise eyes. Only 21 months younger than his brother, he immediately embraced the true understanding of wisdom required to peacefully make his way with honor through this world while bringing it to anyone who would come in contact with him.

2004 my third miracle entered the world a week after his due date. This boy came out with smiling eyes that were a direct window to his sincerely contagious heart and soul. Cheerful was the first thing that came to my mind. This boy was going to bring cheer to the world, the youngest of my three sons, was ready to blaze his own path from the start.

* * * *

2005- 2008

We moved into our new home. We built which was seven miles from the house we were living in across from a family with four kids staggered in age with ours. The husbands became very good buddies, playing softball together. A few weeks after we moved into our new home, the phone rang.

"___was killed in a car accident last night. I'm going over there." that really shook any foundation we might've had in our marriage at this point.

The next Father's Day the boys and I went to Kansas City to their grandpa because their dad (my husband) left us for a fundraiser in support of his friend's wife. She was flooded with her own family support but he left us anyways. I was told by many people in the area that and my husband was seen many days leaving her house on the other side of town.

* * * *

"What are these I yell up to the second story from the driveway." I hear the front door lock. He stands at window laughing as I am pounding on front door, holds the phone up for my Grandparents to hear while he is telling them to hear how crazy I am. He glares with a snicker.

"Why do you have all these Sports illustrated Swimsuit editions in your car?" He takes boys upstairs and locks them in the bedroom while mocking me.

"Hello, I am locked out of my house... I cry into the phone when the 911 operator picks up the phone". As I hand up I hear the door creak as my little Tait runs out in his pull-up. "I'm going with my momma".

* * * *

Within the next year, I take it to heart and wear every emotion on my sleeve I hear- "you're putting on some pounds."

"you're too skinny you need to put on meat"
"You can't give kids choices."
"You don't know anything about working hard."
"Your parents raised you wrong"
"I need to break you down and then build you up the way you should be" "I thought you were a trophy wife"

One drink feels so good. Blocks out the comments that make me feel so worthless.

"Why can't you just be like the other wives and moms just buy the team shirts the company sells." This year it was a red team and orange team and blue team. The Ralph Lauren hats I handpicked for each of the boys ball seasons were currently being embroidered with the boys" numbers. Deep depression sets in - I feel like a failure. I don't even understand how these other wives around here think.

One drink, two drinks, three drinks don't think - block it out

* * * *

2008-2009

Trae's baptism: "My mom and I would read the Bible every day and talk about Jesus." This was the last event we would ever attend as a family unit.

* * * *

I moved out to a house around the corner from our family home. Dancing in the kitchen to "Party in the USA" with the boys in our new temporary home (I had 70% custody) were the days I lived for - but the blocks of time I had to live without them increased ANXIETY'S influence and control over me. My whole being ached without my boys.

* * * *

Court deposition-did you pay to have her runoff the road?" my lawyer questioned him. He looked at his lawyer, "Do I have to answer that?" his lawyer nodded. "Yes but I don't know if he actually ran her off the road."

"Did you lock the meat in the freezer so she couldn't cook dinner until you got home?"

"Yes because I didn't want her to take the meat." Both attorneys' eyebrows raised in bewilderment.

Over the next two years, I was harassed in the middle of the night by his friends, the "good ole boy" police officers, after waking up to a knock on my door. There were hospital visits, sprained ankles and panic attacks. It took a year to get the divorce through because he would not sign his name. My sons lost most of their childlike childhood to an eight year custody battle and their respect for me dwindled as I drank to handle ANXIETY who decided to introduce DEPRESSION to me.

* * * *

Come here go away
Come here go away
They always say
Come here
Oh, wait a minute
- no —-
Just – go away

They learned to betray
In just this way
Leave it, just leave it –
Leave your ego – – at the door,
then hit the floor
BAMM
Need I say more?

Oh, please señor commander
You have the heavy hand
My disgrace is your win
At the race you claim is no sin.

New game - new race
His head, so close it teeters to implode when she asks
Commander, sir may I please have more -
I left my ego at the door.

You might want that shard with which you stabbed me so hard.
It's outside the door where I asked for some more.

Excitedly, he runs, so surely not to bore and down on his face it tore- my
ego forgot to stay put as directed instead it thought only suggested.

Oh, my what a disgrace, that face that splattered and shattered upon the
shard that he killed from- come here - go away - she beamed to completion.

* * * *

2017

I set off on a journey chasing Freedom to try to find her. It was an
attempt to permanently stomp out my bully ANXIETY.

Do I regret standing up for myself after misinterpreted events? Hell no
do I regret handling things my way finally? Absolutely not! Do I regret
leading my stalker away from my family, driving across the country,

running up and down the coast of California? No way! This monster would show up in the middle of the night while I was sleeping in my car. Finally, one chilly evening, he decided the taunting was not enough and kidnap me.. At about two in the morning I found myself sitting in the passenger seat of my car stopped in the middle of the street in the San Francisco tenderloin district. I looked behind me to see a gun being pulled on my kidnapper. Do I wish I would've made a decision which would have taken his life? Sometimes... but I swear my guardian angel made the smart decision for me!

I'm happy with taking a stand and protecting myself and others, even when I take the fall I'm building my train and sometimes even salvaging some of the wreckage from the past I leave some cars behind I repair some cars I built new ones.

* * * *

Dark deliberations stop the activations

Obstructed into oblivion, plummeting down down down into the Wizards instructions. Masked behind the curtain it's certain- Disdainful communication became futile - we all skip and repeat bouncing back onto the Highway to Hell - re-do requested every single time (such a rhyme) trudging nudging and sludging regretfully back up the hill... the mountain, Jack and Jill take a pill or so I thought. Caged by darkness, trapped by tacky teachings of those who proclaimed to fit the bill with slight alterations - borrowing time its narrowing the harrowing feats seen lost in the past—but- maybe -your truth is not our truth - and so the path divides to get the good - the win- the victory whose only sin is the path chosen to get to an end. it's all for the good they recite- but the mark is missed when control spins into obstruction -abduction of free will with frighted white hoods for the good those small cages roll Down the dark into no escape to only find blood on the other side of the gate. The tunnel closes - the mine collapses- wrong train -no rain to water the grass which used to cover your ass.

Bound by the chains that sing the song of lonely regret the sun fades to cold. Sweeping away the rot of the cynical misinterpretation of syndicated spite.

Last train went out at dawn for those who once stood for an illegitimate cause. Our cages are open - we keep the blinds open and always had faith that our time was near for sincere release of fear.

* * * *

2023

After a long drawn out drive to an Austin suburb I reached the Stanley home. I had not seen the Stanley's for over a decade but they had been my first employer after finishing my Masters in Education. I worked for them up to the day before I went into labor with my first born son. They slid into a very valued place in my life as my Christian mentors. {Sidenote: Eight years after making a decision to stay home with my boys and resigning as the assistant director of education for Sylvan Learning Center, as life so mischievously handcrafts our pieces together causing us to stand back, rub our eyes and let out a gasp, "What?" ... My first born son requested that Jack Stanley be the person to baptize him. Trae was in the third grade. Jack had been his Sunday school teacher for a few years. Things began to get very rocky in the family dynamic between his dad and I the year leading up to his baptism. His dad continued to be controlling and self-centered. I was spiraling down into the abyss of depression. I was fighting hard every day to cope with the nonexistent coping skills I had acquired to this point in life. I had three beautiful boys who were my every breath. Trae and I read passages in the Bible and talked about them in the afternoon when his little brothers were sleeping. The road our family was on quickly became jagged and treacherous and my brave boy began to take the weight on his shoulders and watching out for his younger brothers decided it was time to be baptized. Unfortunately, but maybe not so coincidentally, his dad received the divorce papers in the mail, the same day.

2pm - I was standing across from my husband in our driveway. We built the house two years before on ten acres of land. A few hours before the baptism was to begin my husband (at the time) had been served divorce papers. After falling into a deep depression and learning that I had very poor coping skills, and after many attempts too get my husband to attend counseling sessions I had succumbed to the fact that I would quite possibly die if I could not remove myself from a very unhealthy situation, which I also, unfortunately, continued to exacerbate while floundering around, like a fish out of water, trying to find some grounding. As court procedures and the legal three ring circus mumbo-jumbo go, no one could have predicted when exactly the papers would announce their arrival in the mail.

"I will make sure you never see our boys or a penny from me" is what he promised me just two hours before ours son's baptism.}

Heading to Austin. I Felt safe at the Stanley home. I felt a sense of belonging and friendship and healthy guidance. I was excited and agreed to travel to the state where "Everything's bigger" (even though, as for location, I feel much more at home in the more liberal - surfer girl state of California). Ha! Thinking that my purpose, alongside seeing good friends, was to see if my "Coaching Teens To Success" business might mesh with their coaching business, little did I know my life would be transformed after two days of coaching with my mentor Jack. During one of those sessions I got to acknowledge and name the person I was at different points in my life. Freedom Princess Timid- Alpha Me - The future Alpha Princess- Who do I aspire to be?- Who is my goal person? It gave me the chance to acknowledge, embrace, vocally and visually name and observe the strengths and weaknesses of my "SuperMe". I realized that the following events taught me that I like being a princess but I need to throw in some healthy resilient Alpha: Having someone pay to have me run off the road, my deficit in coping skills, my inability to stand up to controlling people in a healthy way, stalked and followed up and down the coast of California, kidnapped, saving the life of my stalker, surprising a guy who tried to rob me when I turned around with a knife (never threaten a lady who is bending over to get something from her back seat thinking she is helpless) letting my heart lead and trying to help young adults stop using meth, losing my boys' trust.

I refuse to be a sellout. I'm not letting them put me on their train. I choose to grow my glow over being the status quo. Fear turns people into controlling greed mongers, haters, toxic people who spread their ooze to others.

* * * *

2024

Do I regret taking a leap of faith to move to Hilton head, South Carolina when some thought I shouldn't? It was the best decision of my life. I made that decision on my own. I did it my way. I blocked out naysayers. The healing comes full circle. Do I regret meeting friends on the internet from Africa and other countries? Ras Panto-from across the world. DJ reminding me that I am not only good, but I can give inspiration across the world. Cyber friends... Some are scams, some are real. Rock Candy at the Big Bamboo bringing together strangers who find happiness and peace on the island.

The last seven-year period of my life, I can only describe as a dichotomy of experiences that got caught in the crossfire. The outcome of their ricochet has defied gravity and the laws of physics. The age old question, does good always overcome evil? My answer is yes, when the heart is good.

Four weeks ago I was re-baptized in the ocean. I'm working for a fitness studio and started my own fitness consultant business. I'm living life on my terms in full faith. I finally made it back on my path to who I was created to be ... academic geek, adventure seeker, fitness and nutrition nut, goodness seeker, gypsy warrior, Mom of three amazing young men - Call me what you will — idealist, vigilante, eccentric... I am what I am.

****

Blazin and Crazin -
Raging White Waves
Raced by Disaster
The Wise SandMaster
Hangs Ten in her Zen.
Slams Challenge with Purpose -
Rises to the Surface -
Stands Strong at the End
Only to transcend

****

My ongoing goal is to align with my purpose, strength and Superpower Me every day. Life is about learning, restructuring and recalibrating to become a better you every day. Life is about respecting and valuing your unique strengths and weaknesses. Life is about pivoting, adjusting your sails to navigate your unique journey to your Authentic Stellar Success.

****

She knew that each obstacle had shaped her into a stronger and more radiant individual than she had ever been before.

The angle she treads,
but can't put to bed
Due to the thread
Which ties and abides by her laugh - distress in the midst of the mess runs rampid but finally Zen
for where she has been -
contagious idealist won't die to the misguided .

I have so many blessings to be thankful for: Family who have supported me through everything, my three amazing sons who have grown into faithful, loving young men with integrity and the fire that has forged me into a strong, resilient woman of faith.

* * * *

I can finally check off each category:

Give Grace to others
Get grace from others
Give grace to self
Dealing with challenges head on
Using healthy coping skills
Grieving
Mourning
Accepting others
Accepting self
Allowing peace

The toughest one and the final piece to put me back on my train: Give Grace to self.

Christine Stow

Empowered Women in Business
Speaker, Author Mentor

https://www.linkedin.com/in/christinestow/
https://www.facebook.com/christine.stow.1
https://www.instagram.com/christineastow
https://www.christinestow.com.au/
https://www.youtube.com/@empoweredwomeninbusiness23

Christine Stow is an Inspirational Speaker, Author, Mentor. She is a winner of International Stevie Women in Business Award for Empowered Women in Business. Life was going well for Christine – From working in Forensic Laboratory to moving to National Sales Medical – she took sales from $200k to $1Million in 3 years. She was on a corporate trajectory flying around the world until she found something wrong with her daughter at three months of age.

She reinvented herself: completed her MBA, stood in a Federal and State Election, elected to council, set up a special school, a café for people with disabilities and support groups for carers. From Carer to Councillor, now Inspirational speaker. Now she Empowers Women who are on a Mission, Vision & purpose to Light the pathway to Live their DREAM and PURPOSE.

She's Not Meeting Her Milestones

By Christine Stow

A story of one mother's love overcomes the barriers and social norms to accept what she cannot change and rise to lead anyway...

"She's not meeting her milestones..."

Those five words uttered by the Child and Maternal Health nurse still ring in my ears today, along with the emotion of helplessness and unknown that floods into the pit of my stomach. The turning point in my life.

It was our three-month visit. I knew the nurse was working really hard, working overtime, to get my beautiful baby to follow that toy. Following the toy would signify my baby was tracking normal development. It wasn't to be.

As I sat staring off into the distance...those words:

What did they mean?
What would my life look like?
What was the future for my three-month-old daughter?
What would the future look like for us as a family?

The pall of grey clouds hung over me while I pondered my coffee with another mum who was on the same journey as me. A mum from my new mum's group. Both of us, a bit older and with our second child. My journey was about to take a totally different turn to hers.

We were referred to a pediatrician. I had to go home to share the news with my husband. That didn't go well. "Who's saying there is something wrong with my child?" he demanded.

I probably felt something not quite right early on. She had been jumpy right after delivery. I asked at the first meeting with the CMHN, but they assured me it was nothing to be concerned about this early.

Then there was the six-week time, she stopped feeding and just went "blank." I would learn these to be seizures—epilepsy.

From that day of the consultation, I was slung into a world of doctors, pediatricians, health professionals, para-health professionals, occupational therapists, speech therapists, dietitians... on it went. I counted 14 health professionals involved in my daughter's life before she was one. It was like being slung into a pinball machine or a merry-go-round I could not get off.

That was 24 years ago.

Where I Come From

At that time in my life, I was on a corporate trajectory. My husband and I were renovating an inner city double front of a Victorian house.

We both had company cars.

Corporate roles with titles—he was state manager, and I was national sales manager for medical supplier. High-flying roles.

Imyjen was our second daughter.

I returned to work pretty soon after I had my first daughter. I planned to get straight back into work after Imyjen: I organised care and a return to work date. I was going to juggle and have it all.

That wasn't to be.

Now, I couldn't imagine how that was going to work with all the appointments and possible surgeries, and still, we didn't know what was wrong. We didn't know the prognosis, and we didn't have a diagnosis.

A pediatrician said to me at one stage: "You'll feel so much better once you get a diagnosis." My response: "Why? She'll still be the same person, the same baby with a diagnosis."

She's never really had a definitive diagnosis. It's not cerebral palsy, they mused, because she would be floppy. She is not floppy. It could be arthrogryposis, they said. Ultimately, they settled on stiff muscle syndrome: Schwartz-Jampel syndrome. To which I often get: "She what... Can you spell that, please..."

Getting Back Into Life

Her early years went from doctor to doctor, appointment to appointment, like an Endless Sea of How Am I Ever Gonna Get Out of This...

This wasn't what I had planned my life to look like. To make it worse, I'd suffered from anxiety, agoraphobia, and depression.

I'm not particularly religious, but I swore at God and told him he gave her to the wrong mother... Surely, you don't know what you're doing? Surely, God knows better.

But I was wrong!

I thought disability wasn't for me. I'd watch other parents pushing wheelchairs and think: that's not in my future. Little did I know.

Into Child Care

Imyjens care team, the professionals involved in her care, suggested she go to child care... Um, what? Leave her? Let her be with people who don't know her? Well, I guess they were the professionals who knew better than me.

So the day came to leave her at childcare.

Leaving my older daughter had been simple. Pack up the bag, a few nappies, clothes, whatever she needs for the day, and hand her over.

Not so simple for Imyjen.

We integrated slowly into childcare.

I dropped her off for only an hour. I drove around in circles, not knowing what to do with myself.

You don't realize when you have a child with special needs how closely they are pinned to your hip for appointment after appointment.

She actually enjoyed it and did quite well with other children. Joining in on the games and eating snacks as all the children did.

Whaaaat? The child carers reported to me one day that Imyjen had enjoyed snacking on biscuits like all the other children! I was alarmed. I had only ever given her smooth liquid food. But I realised she was being pushed, and I was too for her to be like all the other children. They also reported that Imyjen was curious and would look quizzically at the other children when they were crying: Like what's wrong with you? She's quite a sticky nose and loves to see what's going on.

Imyjen went on to enjoy childcare. She learnt a lot and integrated with the other children. She was by all accounts popular. Child carers reported she had fans who would sit by her side and play with her toys, and children who might not so readily engage with others. I think the fact that she is a gentle soul and was stuck in one place was appealing to some of the children who felt safe playing with her toys.

She joined her sister at childcare later on, who was very protective of her. She would not let other children play with her as she was "my sister." But Imyjen did get a lot out of attending childcare. Unfortunately, as time went on, the gap between where she was and the "normal" children became more obvious.

A Job & State Election

Now that Imyjen was in childcare, I felt that I might be able to work, something that seemed impossible going through the diagnosis.

I felt that I didn't know about disability, so I looked for a role in disability so that I could learn more. I gained a role as coordinator for the Northern Region Disability Network, where I was able to double the engagement and membership by running events and listening to the stakeholders: people with disabilities, carers like me, organisational providers, and government representatives.

As I left the role, my manager remarked that I had done a good job despite not having "disability experience." Organisational experience, he meant. But what allowed me to do a GREAT job (and I did!) was my transferable skills as a State and National manager in medical sales: my skills in listening to people.

At the time, as the Disability Coordinator, I came to the attention of people who were setting up a political party to lobby for better services for people with disabilities and their carers. They were at the forefront of what is now NDIS (National Disability Insurance Scheme), which provides services for people with disabilities in Australia. I was of interest to them as I had a profile across the northern metropolitan region of Melbourne in disability.

Initially, my (now ex) husband and I discussed it and said no. It's too much on our family. But then something happened that galvanized my determination, and I said: "That's it! I'm gonna stand!" And I stood in the 2006 State election with my (now ex) husband's blessing to his credit.

We didn't get anyone elected, but it really got the campaign rolling. In 2007, it ramped up, and in 2013, NDIS was established to support Australians with disabilities to live their best lives.

Later, I was asked to stand in the local government election, which I did in 2012 with no expectation of anything other than I would stand and campaign for people with disabilities and carers. But in 2014, fate changed my direction, and I was elected on a countback to local government! During that time, I was able to achieve great things, like getting a special school for children with disabilities and a cafe for people with disabilities to be employed in. Both projects I am very proud of.

My Books

After I was elected to government, I was slated to attend a retreat where I would write a book. The 48-hour Author Retreat where I wrote my story titled *Not Just Imyjen's Mother*. It turned out, it wasn't about the book, and it wasn't about what I learned on that weekend. What it really became about was a watershed moment for me. It was the first time that I'd left Imyjen for that length of time with support workers. Previously I'd only left her short periods of time with certain people who could care for her. My book was published in 2015. I had the Federal Minister for NDIS and Disabilities launch my book. It gave me authority and recognition for what I had achieved as a carer and in my political journey.

From the moment I started writing, it was my dream to put together a compilation of carer stories—stories like mine, because I wanted other carers to get recognition and acknowledgement for what they had to offer just like I did. You see, it is my belief, that we all have talents, and we all have gifts to offer no matter what we are going through, or how tough our challenges might be. And I wanted to see to it that others would be able to do what I had done with my book.

This was my dream, but I put it off. I didn't make it happen.
I let it go.
I didn't get around to it.
I never had the time.
I never had the money.
And how was I ever going to get carers together to put their stories to paper?

THEN, in 2022, my best friend, who'd walked the journey of disability with me since our daughters were 18 months old, suddenly passed away. I always imagined she would be one of my authors, but now she was gone.

That was a big kick in A** I needed to get me going.
Why had I put it off?
What else was I waiting for?

Who else would not be there to be part of it?
Don't do that! If you have a dream...

DO IT! DO IT NOW!

So, I set about putting together a compilation of carer stories.
I started interviewing carers.
I didn't know what I was looking for.
And I didn't have money either!

But I got started.

I ran podcasts of empowered women in business where they contributed funds for the podcast to the cost of the book. I was able to raise a significant amount to offset the cost of the book production, which was amazing! I'm very proud of what I achieved. And more carers learnt about the book and wanted to be part of it. The podcasts were like a marketing opportunity as well as raising funds.

Once I got started, I got clearer on what I wanted the book to be about. I wanted it to be an inspiration for others who didn't think they could achieve anything... And so it is!

It snowballed. More carers got on board, and more women contributed through the podcasts. It was amazing! We launched in September 2023: *Stories from the Heart: The Carers Journey* and sold out of books on the night!

Key takeaways from my experiences:

1. If you want something: Dream it! You can make it possible
2. Believe it's possible
3. No matter how big your challenge: There is a way
4. Overcoming your challenges gives you the keys, the pathway that allows you to help others
5. Create the steps. TAKE ACTION. You can do it! It's possible

Through overcoming my challenges to:

- Write two books
- Stand in elections
- Set up a YouTube channel
- Run podcasts
- Set up a school for children with disabilities and a cafe for people with disabilities to run
- Get elected to Government

Being a carer for my daughter has allowed me to now help other women overcome challenges, map out their dreams, and create a life they love.

Now, 24 years later, Imyjen does not walk or talk, she is no longer able to eat food and is fed via a tube (PEG) in her stomach. She is like an 8-month-old baby; I need to anticipate her every need. NDIS provides her support that helps us live life as fully as we can. I've just been elected to government again, where I can have an impact. I can say that I truly rose to lead as a result of the challenges I faced. If not for Imyjen, I would not be on the path I am on. I don't know what other path I might have taken. I don't think I would have been elected to government, but I can't know. What I know is that I can say that I truly rose to lead as a result of the challenges I faced.

Imyjen gave me an excuse to step off my corporate trajectory, stop work, and smell the roses. To see things differently and do things differently. It might not be the pathway I had mapped out before I had my children... But boy, it's been a huge journey. I never imagined that I would be able to work after finding something wrong with her. But because I dreamed I could and I believed I should, I have been able to achieve amazing things I would never have dreamed possible! Now I want to inspire others to have a DREAM, to BELIEVE, and to take ACTION.

And you know how I said at the start of this chapter that I spoke with God, the universe, creator, or whatever you call him, and questioned his wisdom in sending Imyjen to me... Well...

I look back and think: Imyjen is still with me. She is MY greatest gift. She is a gift of LOVE. I was trained as part of my job in medical sales to be a public speaker. My skills were listening to people and standing up for them. HE KNEW EXACTLY WHAT HE WAS DOING!

SHE RISES
SHE LEADS
SHE LIVES

***Child and Maternal Health Nurse** is a Nurse practitioner in Australia who tracks infants progress to make sure everything is within normal range

*In Australia the term "**Carer**" is used to describe a person who is family or connection who provides unpaid support for someone who has a disability, aged, frail or who may have a health condition. In other countries they may be referred to as a "Care Giver".

Dashana Jefferies

Founder and CEO of A Passport 2 Breathe

https://www.linkedin.com/in/thedashanajefferies/
https://www.facebook.com/dashana.jefferies
https://instagram.com/thedashanajefferies
https://www.apassport2breathe.com/
https://www.thedashanajefferies.com/

Meet Dashana Jefferies, a trailblazer in AI, mental wellness, and education. As the CEO and founder of A Passport 2 Breathe, she has revolutionized mental health support through innovative AI solutions. Inducted into Marquis Who's Who in America in 2024, Dashana's journey from overcoming depression, anxiety, and PTSD to becoming a leader in her field is truly inspiring.

Her academic achievements are remarkable—she earned a second bachelor's and a master's degree in psychology through accelerated programs and is now pursuing a doctorate in Educational Leadership. Dashana's award-winning books, "365 Intentional Breaths" and "365 Love Letters to the World's Black Kings," offer daily affirmations and strength.

With over 20 years of experience, Dashana is a sought-after speaker and AI consultant known for integrating AI into business and education. Her work inspires and leads conversations on using technology to build a more empathetic and resilient world.

Underneath the Night Sky:
A Journey to the Breaking Point

By Dashana Jefferies

Curled like a forgotten shadow, I did not think I would see another sunrise. Immobilized, an invisible force weighed down every inch of me. My body, my limbs—they were not mine anymore. The crushing weight of despair was suffocating. The concoction of pills and alcohol was supposed to silence it all, to end this relentless pain.

Every breath was a battle, each heartbeat a cruel reminder of my existence. Trapped in an ocean of hopelessness, I genuinely believed there was no escape but one. Isolation wrapped around me like a vice, and betrayal's sting made every passing second an unbearable eternity. The darkness did not just surround me; it had swallowed me whole. I was ready to disappear. As I waited for the abyss, I made a desperate plea to God. If this night did not claim me, I would seek help. It was not merely a plea for survival; it was an acknowledgment that I deserved more than this unending torment.

However, how did I end up here? This is different from where the story began.

The Call That Shattered My World

I received that phone call—the kind no one ever wants. After 2.5 years of what I believed was a loving relationship, I found myself on the other end of the line, listening to a voice that was not his but belonged to his wife of 12 years. The words pierced me like a dagger, unraveling everything I thought I knew about my life.

Our relationship was not a casual fling but a deeply woven tapestry of moments, dreams, and shared futures. He had pursued me relentlessly at the beginning. There was nothing easy about getting with me; that challenge intrigued him even more. When I finally let my guard down, I thought I had found something real.

We were not just dating; we were building a life together. I met his mother in person and would talk to her on the phone—or so I thought. I later discovered it was his cousin I had been speaking to on the phone, a twisted part of his elaborate lie. We spent the holidays together, celebrated my 40th surprise birthday party with my family, and went on vacation. He even attended family weddings with me, blending seamlessly into my life. The week we had our first date, unbeknownst to me, his wife had just given birth.

We looked at rings, discussed our future, and imagined a life built on love and trust. All of it was a lie. His deceit betrayed not just our relationship but also my sense of reality. I was living a nightmare disguised as a dream.

The Descent Into Darkness

That night, a part of me did die. The version that had carried unbearable sadness and anxiety ceased to exist. What emerged from the wreckage was a delicate resolve, a commitment to reclaim my life.

I reflected on the promises I had broken to myself over the years. Each one was a betrayal, feeding the cycle of despair. However, this promise felt different. It was born out of desperation but also a deep-seated desire to live, to find meaning again. I did not want to be left in pain; I wanted to grow and bloom.

The morning light found me alive, though barely. There was a strange serenity in surviving. I realized that the fight was not over—it was just beginning. The journey ahead seemed daunting, but I felt a glimmer of possibility for the first time in a long while.

After that phone call, the weight of my world came crashing down. Every moment we had shared, every word of love he had spoken, felt tainted. The betrayal shattered more than my heart; it tore through my sense of self-worth and trust.

I spiraled into a pit of despair, unable to reconcile the man I loved with the man who had lied to me. My mind replayed every memory, every touch, every promise, trying to find the clues I had missed. The guilt of not seeing the signs, of not protecting myself, consumed me. The mask of strength I had worn for so long began to crack under the weight of this new pain.

That night, overwhelmed by the burden of betrayal and years of unaddressed emotional wounds, I reached my breaking point.

Living with Shadows

Unbeknownst to me, I had been living with clinical depression and anxiety my entire life. The signs were there, but I did not have the words to name them. I always felt a gnawing sense of emptiness, a deep-seated anxiety that kept me striving for perfection and approval. My people-pleasing tendencies were rooted in fear—fear of rejection, fear of abandonment.

I realized that these patterns had shaped every decision, from the relationships I entered to how I managed conflict. I often found myself in relationships with people who mirrored my insecurities. I ignored red flags, clung to the wrong mates, and allowed myself to be hurt, all because I did not believe I deserved better.

My diagnosis, while painful, was illuminating. It explained why I found it hard to speak up for myself, why I could not say no, and why I constantly sought validation from others. His betrayal was the catalyst that forced me to confront these truths.

Missing Red Flags: How They Show Up in Life

Red flags sometimes appear as bold warning signs. Sometimes, they are subtle, woven into the fabric of our daily interactions. In relationships, red flags manifest as small but persistent doubts about a partner's honesty, inconsistencies in their stories, or feelings of unease that we dismiss or rationalize.

In my case, the red flags were there, but I was blind to them. His evasiveness about specific topics, his always-overly-perfect appearance, and the gaps in his story about his family all signaled that something was amiss. However, I ignored them because I wanted to believe in our love.

Missing red flags often stem from a deeper issue: our unresolved traumas and insecurities. When we do not feel worthy of love, we settle for less, convincing ourselves that we do not deserve better. This is why healing from past wounds and building a solid sense of self-worth is crucial.

Trauma's Signals: Recognizing the Signs

Trauma has a way of embedding itself deep within us, showing up in unexpected ways. It can manifest as chronic anxiety, a tendency to overreact or shut down in certain situations, or patterns of self-sabotage. The body keeps score of our pain, even when our minds try to bury it.

For me, the signals were clear in hindsight. I would feel an inexplicable sense of dread before specific conversations, a tightening in my chest when confronted with conflict, or a wave of nausea at the thought of being alone. This was my body's way of telling me that something was wrong, that I needed to pay attention.

Recognizing these signals is the first step toward healing. It requires listening to your body, acknowledging your emotions, and seeking help to process and move through the trauma.

A Whisper in the Void

Amidst the overwhelming sorrow, a fragile spark ignited within me—a faint but persistent voice whispering hope. As I waited for the abyss, I made a desperate plea to the universe. If this night did not claim me, I would seek help. It was not merely a plea for survival but an acknowledgment that I deserved more than this unending torment.

The following day, with the weight of despair still heavy on my chest, I decided. I would not let this betrayal define me. The healing journey would be arduous, but I owed it to myself to try.

The Road to Redemption

True to my word, I stepped into the terrifying world of therapy. Exposing my wounds, confronting my demons—it was the hardest thing I had ever done. However, it was necessary. Diagnosis of clinical depression, PTSD, and anxiety peeled back layers of my existence, revealing truths I had long buried. Therapy became a lifeline, guiding me through the labyrinth of my mind.

Understanding the roots of my pain helped me see my life in a new light. Therapy offered me tools to manage my anxiety, cope with depression, and rebuild my self-esteem. It taught me that my worth was not tied to my ability to endure pain or please others but to my capacity for self-love and authenticity.

Steps to Thriving After Tragedy

1. **Acknowledge the Pain** - The first step is recognizing and accepting the pain. Denying it only prolongs the suffering. Allow yourself to feel the emotions, no matter how overwhelming.
2. **Seek Professional Help** - Therapy can be a notable change. Finding a therapist you trust can help you navigate your complex emotions and challenges. They can provide you with strategies to cope and heal.

3. **Build a Support System** - Surround yourself with people who uplift you. These could be friends, family, or support groups. Knowing you are not alone can provide immense comfort and strength.

4. **Practice Self-Compassion** - Be gentle with yourself. Acknowledge your struggles and celebrate small victories. Self-compassion can be a powerful tool in healing.

5. **Set Small, Achievable Goals** - Focus on what you can control. Set small, daily goals to build confidence and momentum. Every small step forward is progress.

6. **Find Meaning in Your Experience** - Find ways to transform your pain into purpose. Finding meaning can be profoundly healing through advocacy, creative expression, or helping others.

7. **Embrace Vulnerability** - Sharing your story can be a powerful way to heal and connect with others. It allows you to release the burden of secrecy and find solidarity in shared experiences.

8. **Prioritize Self-Care** - Take care of your physical and emotional well-being. Regular exercise, a healthy diet, and adequate sleep can significantly impact mental health.

9. **Engage in Mindfulness Practices** - Techniques like meditation, deep breathing, and yoga can help you stay present and reduce anxiety.

10. **Stay Committed to Your Healing Journey** - Healing is not linear. There will be setbacks, but each step forward is a victory. Stay committed to your journey, knowing that thriving is possible.

Accomplishments Rooted in Resilience

Despite the trauma, or perhaps because of it, I have accomplished what once seemed impossible. I pursued a second bachelor's degree in psychology, completing it in record time and I earned a master's degree in psychology in just 12 weeks, a feat that required immense focus and determination. This accelerated journey was about academic achievement and reclaiming my narrative. Each course and each assignment felt like a step away from the darkness and toward a new purpose.

These were not just degrees—it was validation. It affirmed my ability to rise above my past and transform my experiences into a foundation for a new life.

Now, as a doctoral candidate, I am growing deeper into understanding human behavior and the mind through the studies of Educational Leadership. Within six months, I have made strides that I never thought possible. This journey is about personal growth and contributing to a broader understanding of trauma, resilience, and healing.

Award-Winning Author

The pain and lessons from my experiences also found their way into my writing. I authored two books, *365 Intentional Breaths* and *365 Love Letters to the World's Black Kings* resonating with readers worldwide. These works, born from my healing process, have won awards, and become examples of hope for others navigating their storms.

Writing became a therapeutic outlet to channel my pain into something constructive and empowering. It allowed me to connect with others, share my journey, and offer insights that could help them find their paths to healing.

Rising from the Ashes

Therapy was just the beginning of my transformation. It equipped me to rebuild, one step at a time. The pain I had carried became the foundation for a new purpose. I dedicated myself to mental health advocacy, creating tools like the A Passport 2 Breathe app and penning words to uplift others.

Sharing my journey with others was both cathartic and empowering. I realized my story could be a flashlight of hope for those still in the darkness. By being vulnerable and admitting my struggles, I gave others permission to do the same.

Through my advocacy, I connected with individuals from all social classes. Each story I heard reinforced the universality of pain and the resilience of the human spirit. I was no longer alone in my journey; I was part of a community committed to healing and growth.

Today, I am a survivor and storyteller, sharing my journey to inspire and empower. My message is clear: Even in the darkest night, there is light to guide your back.

A Call to Courage

If you find yourself in despair, remember this: Vulnerability is strength. Seeking help is not surrender; it is a declaration of your worth. Your journey may be fraught with challenges, but every step forward is a testament to your resilience.

Embrace your scars, paint your story with new colors, and know that healing is possible. Together, we can rise, heal, and thrive.

Phuoc Anne Nguyen, PharmD, MS, BCPS,FTSHP

Franbyte Business Consulting-Southwest
Franchise Business Coach

https://www.linkedin.com/in/phuocannenguyen/
https://www.youtube.com/@DrAnneleads
https://www.instagram.com/dranneleads/
https://linktr.ee/DrAnneLeads
https://www.startfranchisetoday.com/

Dr. Anne Nguyen, also known as Ms. Impact, is a franchise consultant dedicated to helping aspiring entrepreneurs—especially high-achieving women—unlock business ownership through franchising. With over 10 years of experience in leadership and business, Anne combines her expertise to guide high performers toward franchise opportunities that align with their passions, values, and financial goals. As a pharmacist by trade, entrepreneur by nature, and coach by choice, Anne's mission is to empower others to succeed on their own terms. She offers personalized consulting at no cost, helping aspiring entrepreneurs navigate the world of franchising to build impactful, lasting businesses. Outside of work, Anne is a mom of two and a national parks enthusiast, aiming to visit 50 parks by age 50. Ready to turn your entrepreneurial dreams into reality? Connect with Anne today to explore your options.

Forging Her Way:
From Barriers to Bold Leadership in Business

By Phuoc Anne Nguyen, PharmD, MS, BCPS,FTSHP

In every woman's heart lies an ember—a quiet spark yearning to ignite into something extraordinary. That spark whispered to me long before I knew the road I would walk. I come from a world where women were expected to be silent pillars, holding up others' dreams, not chasing their own. Yet, here I am, a woman who stepped into the light, navigating challenges, building businesses, and making an impact.

This chapter is a love letter to the dreamers, the risk-takers, and the determined souls ready to chart their path. It begins with a simple truth: *the first step matters most.*

From a New Land to a New Life

When my family moved to the United States, I was nine years old. We left behind a life we knew well for one that promised hope but offered uncertainty. We arrived with suitcases filled with clothes and a mind brimming with dreams, yet the first day of school became a day I'll never forget.

I sat at my desk in a classroom full of strangers, their words buzzing around me like bees I couldn't understand. I didn't know a single word of English, and that silence felt like an enormous weight pressing on my chest. *How could I learn? How could I belong?*

It wasn't just the language that was unfamiliar; it was everything. The food tasted strange, the customs felt foreign, and even the smiles seemed somehow different. At recess, other kids played tag while I stood alone by the swings, a spectator in my own life. But within me was a quiet determination, a belief that one day, I wouldn't just watch—I would join.

Practical Strategy: Adapting to the Unfamiliar

1. **Embrace the Beginner Mindset:** Start small. Focus on learning one new word, skill, or cultural nuance each day. Small wins build momentum.

2. **Seek Out Role Models:** Watch and learn from those who have adapted successfully. In my case, TV shows and observing classmates were invaluable.

3. **Celebrate Progress:** Acknowledge every breakthrough, no matter how minor. For me, it was answering a question in class, even with trembling hands.

The Fire of Adaptation

Adapting wasn't a choice; it was survival. Each evening, I sat with a dictionary at the kitchen table, painstakingly translating homework assignments word by word. Television became my secret weapon—reruns of sitcoms and cartoons taught me not just English, but the rhythm of American life.

But there's one part of adapting that isn't always talked about: the fear.

I was painfully shy. I didn't speak up in class, not because I didn't know the answer, but because I was terrified of being judged. My accent, the way I pronounced certain words, the way I strung together sentences—it all felt like it set me apart, not in a good way. I spent most of my school days blending into the background, hoping not to be noticed. Even outside of class, I avoided conversation with peers for fear they'd hear the hesitation in my voice and judge me.

For years, this fear kept me locked in a shell of my own making. It wasn't just the language barrier; it was the constant worry that I didn't belong, that my voice wasn't good enough. And so, I stayed silent, watching the world move around me while I stood on the sidelines.

My breakthrough moment came when I finally answered a question in class. My voice was shaky, my accent heavy, but my teacher smiled and said, "Good job." That moment, small as it was, lit a tiny flame of confidence in me.

As the years passed, that flame grew. I began to excel in school, even winning awards for my writing—an irony not lost on the girl who once couldn't string a sentence together. But the journey wasn't smooth. There were times I felt like an outsider, caught between two worlds: the culture of my family and the expectations of this new country.

Practical Strategy: Building Confidence Through Action

1. **Take Small Risks Daily:** Push yourself to speak up in one conversation, meeting, or classroom daily. Each time you do, you build confidence.

2. **Reframe Fear:** Instead of thinking, "What if they judge me?" ask, "What if I inspire them?"

3. **Journal Your Wins:** Write down every moment where you pushed past fear and succeeded. Revisit these entries whenever self-doubt creeps in.

The Unexpected Beginning

I didn't think college was possible. My family's finances were tight, and the idea of higher education seemed as distant as a star. Even though I was a high achiever in high school, the thought of attending college was a luxury we couldn't afford. I was prepared to settle for what seemed realistic—work a steady job, contribute to the household, and let go of my dream to do more.

But sometimes, life has a way of surprising us. It was my high school counselor, a kind yet persistent woman, who planted a seed I hadn't dared to imagine. "You're meant for college," she told me one day, her eyes steady with conviction. "You just have to believe it first."

It was the first time someone had looked at me and seen potential I couldn't yet see in myself. That moment shifted something inside me. I began to wonder: *What if she's right?* What if I said yes to myself before the world said yes?

Then, a lifeline appeared: the Gates Millennium Scholarship.

Winning that scholarship was one of the most triumphant moments of my life. I'll never forget reading the acceptance letter, my hands trembling and tears streaming down my face. *I did it.*

A Survive or Sink Moment

Moving to a college town was both exhilarating and terrifying. I left the safety net of home, the familiarity of my family, and arrived in a place where I didn't know a single soul. The first few weeks were a blur of loneliness, overwhelming coursework, and a creeping sense of isolation.

When I started my educational journey, it wasn't smooth sailing. Early in my first semester in one of my hardest science classes, a professor told me outright, "You don't belong here." Those words crushed me.

For days, I questioned everything: Was he right? Was I an imposter? I'd sit in my dorm room at night, thinking, *How am I going to do this?*

But then, something clicked. I realized that this was my chance to start fresh. No one here knew me as the shy girl who never spoke. I could rewrite my story, but only if I chose to. I decided to let his words fuel me. I worked harder than ever.

It was my survive or sink moment.

The first step was forcing myself to speak. In class, I raised my hand even when my heart raced and my palms sweated. At first, my voice trembled, and I stumbled over words, but each time, I grew a little braver. In the cafeteria, I started sitting with people I didn't know, pushing past the awkwardness of introducing myself.

One of the hardest moments came during a group project in my freshman year. My group was debating ideas, and I had one that I thought could work. The old me would have stayed silent, but this time, I spoke up. When my group agreed with my suggestion and incorporated it, I felt a surge of pride. *My voice mattered.*

Practical Strategy: Using Doubt as Fuel

1. **Turn Criticism into Action:** When someone doubts you, channel that energy into proving them wrong—not for them, but for yourself.

2. **Set Milestones:** Break down your goals into smaller steps. Celebrate each one as proof that you're capable.

3. **Build a Support Network:** Surround yourself with people who believe in you and encourage your growth.

Finding My Confidence

Over time, I realized that most people weren't judging me nearly as much as I was judging myself. My accent? It was just a part of who I was. My perspective? It was unique and valuable, precisely because of the experiences that shaped it.

College became a proving ground for me. Each time I pushed myself out of my comfort zone, I discovered something new about my strength and resilience. By the time I graduated, I wasn't just surviving—I was thriving.

That moment of adaptation wasn't just about learning English or navigating a new culture. It was about reclaiming my voice. I realized that the greatest barrier wasn't my accent or my background; it was the fear I had allowed to take root. Once I let that fear go, the possibilities became limitless. By the time I graduated college, I did so with top honors—a direct challenge to anyone who doubted me.

Believing Before You See It

Melinda Gates once said, *"A woman with a voice is, by definition, a strong woman. But the search to find that voice can be remarkably difficult."* For me, that search began with the realization that I needed to believe in possibilities before they materialized.

Taking the first step wasn't easy.

The First Job: Lessons in Grit and the Spark of Entrepreneurship

It was my freshman year at the University of Texas at Austin, and like many students, I needed a job to help cover my expenses. My first job wasn't glamorous—it was as a gym attendant. At first glance, it seemed like a simple enough role, but it would teach me lessons that stayed with me long after my time at the gym ended.

The shifts were grueling. My day started at 4 a.m., when most of the campus was still asleep. I'd unlock the doors, set up the equipment, and greet the early risers who made fitness their priority before the sun even peeked over the horizon. After my shift, I'd rush to attend classes, trying my best to stay alert despite the exhaustion that clung to me like a shadow. Then, in the evening, I'd return to close the gym at 10 p.m., tidying up the space and locking up for the night.

It was a schedule that tested my limits. Most days, I felt like I was running on fumes, juggling school, my job, and the constant pressure to succeed. But here's the thing about challenges: they build grit.

The Lesson of Grit

Waking up at 4 a.m. wasn't just about getting to work on time—it was about discipline. I learned that sometimes, success means showing up, even when every fiber of your being begs you to hit snooze. It wasn't easy to focus during the lectures after an early morning shift or to study for exams in the small windows of free time I had. But I knew what was at stake.

The gym became my training ground—not just for physical fitness, but for mental resilience. I learned how to push through fatigue, stay focused on my goals, and keep moving forward even when the road felt impossibly hard.

The Encounter That Changed Everything

One quiet morning, as I was wiping down the equipment, a man in a casual workout outfit entered the gym. He was a regular—someone I'd seen countless times but never spoken to beyond a polite "Good morning." That day, however, he struck up a conversation.

"You're here every day," he observed. "Early mornings, late nights. That's impressive."

"Thank you," I said, feeling a mix of pride and exhaustion.

"Can I give you some advice?" he asked, leaning casually against the treadmill.

"Of course," I said, curious.

He smiled and said, "You're trading your time for money right now. And there's nothing wrong with that—most people start there. But if you want to create real freedom for yourself, think about this: How can you make money while you sleep?"

I was taken aback. I'd never thought about money in those terms before. Up until that point, my focus had been on working hard, earning a paycheck, and making ends meet. That was what I was taught all my life. The idea that money could work for me, instead of the other way around, was revolutionary.

"Think about ownership," he continued. "Business. Investments. Those are the paths to freedom. You've got the grit—now start thinking about how to use it to build something bigger."

The Spark of Entrepreneurship

That conversation planted a seed in my mind. For the rest of my shift, I couldn't stop thinking about his words. *How can I make money while I sleep?*

At the time, I didn't have a concrete plan, but the idea of entrepreneurship began to take root. I started paying attention to the business world, reading books and articles about successful entrepreneurs. I realized that the skills I was developing—discipline, resilience, and work ethic—were the same skills that could help me one day create something of my own.

There were nights when exhaustion felt like a permanent shadow. But there were also glimmers of hope—an encouraging professor, a breakthrough exam score, and the growing sense that I was carving a path not just for myself, but for others who might follow. Lastly, that man in the gym didn't just give me advice; he gave me a new lens through which to view my future.

Practical Strategy: Turning Grit into Growth

1. **Embrace the Hard Work:** Use your current job as a training ground for discipline and resilience.

2. **Learn from Everyone:** Every person you meet can teach you something. Ask questions, listen, and absorb their wisdom.

3. **Start Exploring:** Research ways to build passive income or start a side business. Think about how your skills can be turned into opportunities.

Be the First

Kamala Harris said, *"You may be the first to do many things, but make sure you're not the last."* These words resonate deeply with me because being the first is not just a personal achievement—it's an act of service.

I was the first in my family to attend college. The first to become a pharmacist.

In pharmacy school, I encountered another pivotal moment. I wanted to apply for a leadership scholarship, but when I approached a professor for advice, she said, "You're not ready yet. Maybe wait another year."

I felt defeated, but something in me wouldn't let go of the idea. I sought a second opinion from another professor, a mentor who I always sought for life and professional advice.

"Ready?" he said with a laugh. "Of course, you're ready. Don't let anyone tell you otherwise."

He wrote me a glowing letter of recommendation, and I got the scholarship, which also helped me land a leadership role at a national level.

That leadership role became one of the most transformative experiences of my life. It taught me that belief in yourself is more powerful than anyone else's doubts.

Practical Strategy: Asking the Right Questions

1. **Seek Second Opinions:** If someone doubts you, find another perspective. The right mentor can make all the difference.

2. **Prepare Yourself:** Build the skills and knowledge you need to feel confident stepping into leadership roles.

3. **Take the Leap:** Even if you're unsure, apply for the role, project, or opportunity. Growth happens outside your comfort zone.

Leadership Through Service

Pharmacy was where I found my voice as a leader. Rising through the ranks, I discovered a passion for building programs that served both patients and professionals. Leadership, I realized, wasn't about authority—it was about *service.*

John Maxwell captures this beautifully: *"A leader is one who knows the way, goes the way, and shows the way."* Whether it was mentoring a new pharmacist, streamlining operations, or advocating for patient care, I learned that true leadership is rooted in empathy and action.

The Continued Entrepreneurial Spark

That job as a gym attendant may have been my first, but it became the foundation for something much greater. It didn't just pay the bills—it set me on the path to dreaming of a life where I could create, lead, and inspire others.

So, here's my advice to anyone reading this: Don't underestimate the power of your first job. It might seem like a small step, but it could lead you to a life you never imagined. The key is to approach it with an open mind, a strong work ethic, and a willingness to learn from every person and experience you encounter.

That man in the gym probably doesn't even remember our conversation, but I carry his words with me to this day. They remind me to think bigger, to work smarter, and to always, always dream of what's possible.

Reflecting on that gym experience and my upbringing with my dad as a small business owner having a mechanic shop, I realized that business was always in my DNA. My parents and siblings, who have been small business owners, taught me that success isn't about shortcuts—it's about grit, resilience, and adaptability. While I thrived in my pharmacy career, I felt the pull of something more.

Franchising entered my life as both a challenge and an opportunity. Becoming a franchising business broker was a way to combine my love for systems with my entrepreneurial roots. But more importantly, it became a platform to empower others.

For aspiring franchise owners, franchising isn't just about running a business—it's about creating freedom, generational wealth, and purpose.

As women, we must believe in ourselves first. We can't wait for permission, validation, or the "perfect moment."

Leadership and entrepreneurship are not reserved for the privileged few. They are for those willing to work, adapt, and take risks.

Lessons Learned

1. **Grit Is Non-Negotiable:** Success requires showing up, even when it's hard, even when you're tired, even when no one is watching.

2. **Every Interaction Matters:** You never know when a conversation can change your perspective—or your life.

3. **Dream Bigger:** It's not enough to work hard; you have to work smart. Start thinking about how to build a life where your money and time work for you, not the other way around.

Practical Strategy: The Power of Affirmations

One of the strategies that carried me through those challenging times was practicing affirmations. Here's how you can start:

1. **Identify Your Fear:** Write down the limiting belief that's holding you back (e.g., "I'm not good enough to start a business").

2. **Flip the Script:** Transform it into a positive affirmation (e.g., "I am capable and ready to lead my own business").

3. **Repeat Daily:** Speak this affirmation to yourself every morning to rewire your mindset.

> *"Your life is your story. Write well. Edit often."*
> —Unknown

A Personal Invitation: Take the First Step Toward Empowerment

The first step is always the hardest—but it's also the most powerful. If you feel that spark inside you—the one that whispers, *You're meant for more*—listen to it.

Take the first step toward your dreams. Whether it's applying for a leadership role, starting your own business, or simply speaking up for yourself, remember: *Believe in yourself first.*

If you're reading this and feel the desire to take control of your own destiny, to build something meaningful for yourself and your family, I invite you to connect with me. Franchise ownership has empowered many individuals to achieve financial independence and create lives filled with purpose and control. Whether you're looking to pivot, build a legacy, or simply explore new opportunities, I'm here to guide you through every step.

Connect with me on LinkedIn, join my newsletter for insights and resources on business ownership and empowerment, and let's explore how franchise ownership can be your path to a brighter future. This journey is about more than business—it's about building a life that aligns with who you truly are. Reach out, and let's walk this path together.

Let's connect and explore how I can guide you on this journey.

- **Linktree: https://linktr.eeDrAnneLeads**
- **Newsletter: Join my newsletter on my website for insights on empowerment, business ownership, and personal growth.**
- **LinkedIn: https://www.linkedin.com/in/phuocannenguyen/**
- **YouTube: https://www.youtube.com/@DrAnneleads**
- **Instagram: https://www.instagram.com/dranneleads/**

Reach out, ask questions, and take the leap. *Your future is waiting. Own it.*

Practical Strategy: Believing in Yourself First - Visualization for Success

Vishen Lakhiani once said, *"You are more powerful than you know, and they fear the day you discover it."* That discovery starts when you say yes to yourself.

1. Close your eyes and picture the life you want—your career, relationships, and daily routines.
2. Break that vision into achievable steps.
3. Take one actionable step toward that vision every day, no matter how small.

Practical Strategy: Assessing Franchise Readiness

If you're considering franchise business ownership, ask yourself:

- Do I thrive in structured environments, or do I prefer full autonomy?
- Can I commit to the financial and time investment required to succeed?
- Does the franchise align with my passions and long-term goals?

Additional Resources for Woman Empowerment and Business Ownership

Empowering women and business owners is my passion. Here are some resources to support your journey:

- **SCORE (Service Corps of Retired Executives):** Free mentorship and tools for aspiring entrepreneurs.
  - **Website**: www.score.org
  - **What it Offers**: SCORE is a nonprofit organization that partners with the U.S. Small Business Administration

(SBA) to provide free, high-quality mentoring and resources for small business owners. It offers one-on-one mentoring from experienced business professionals, live and recorded webinars, workshops, and a vast library of articles and templates.

- **Small Business Administration (SBA):** Resources, loans, and training for small business owners.

    o **Website**: www.sba.gov
    o **What it Offers**: The SBA is a government agency that provides comprehensive support for small businesses. It offers business loans, grant programs, and educational resources, as well as free counseling services through local district offices and partner organizations. The SBA's loan programs, like 7(a) loans and microloans, are especially popular for those seeking funding.

- **Small Business Development Centers (SBDC):** Expert advice and support for entrepreneurs.

    o **Website**: www.sba.gov/local-assistance/find
    o **What it Offers**: SBDCs are a nationwide network of offices that provide free consulting and low-cost training to new and existing small business owners. Supported by the SBA, SBDCs offer services like business plan development, financial planning, and marketing strategies. They also assist with navigating local, state, and federal regulations.

- *"Lean In" by Sheryl Sandberg* – A must-read for women stepping into leadership roles.

- *"Start with Why" by Simon Sinek* – Discover your purpose and lead with intention.

Audrey Dworak

CEO of Your Whole Self Wellness

https://www.facebook.com/YourWholeSelfWellness
https://www.instagram.com/yourwholeselfwellness
https://linktr.ee/healthcoach67
https://yourwholeselfwellness.com/

Audrey Dworak is the CEO of Your Whole Self Wellness and a committed Functional Nutritional Health Coach, Nutritional Therapist, and Culinary Nutritional Expert. With over 14 years of experience, Audrey has dedicated her career to empowering women through Perimenopause and beyond. She provides both virtual and local, in-person coaching to support women in reclaiming their health and vitality. Audrey's expertise lies in balancing hormones, boosting energy, promoting healthy weight loss, and fostering a lifestyle and mindset rooted in wellness. Her holistic approach equips women to overcome wellness challenges, build resilience, and rediscover a sense of wholeness and self-confidence. Audrey's mission is to help her clients reconnect with their true selves and embrace healthier, more fulfilling lives. By tailoring her support to meet each client's unique needs, she ensures they are fully supported on their journey to lasting wellness.

Breaking Free: A Journey of Healing, Strength, and Renewal

By Audrey Dworak

From the outside, my life appeared idyllic: a loving husband, three beautiful children, and a role as a stay-at-home mom tending to my family. It was the picture of suburban bliss, the kind of life that others might envy. But as many women know, appearances can be deceptive. Behind closed doors, I was waging two battles—one within my home and the other within my own body.

For years, I lived in an emotionally abusive marriage with a man whose narcissistic tendencies made life unbearable. His moods swung unpredictably, his words cut deeply, and his gaslighting made me question my own sense of reality. The man I had once thought of as my partner became the very source of my pain. I remember the feeling of walking on eggshells, constantly censoring myself in fear of triggering his anger.

Financially, we were always on the edge. My husband struggled to keep a job, and I, as a stay-at home mom, had no financial independence. The weight of the household fell squarely on my shoulders, from managing scarce resources to nurturing my children, all while enduring his criticism. Every day felt like a battle just to keep our family afloat, and the emotional toll was immense.

As if the strain of my marriage wasn't enough, my body began betraying me in ways I couldn't ignore. In 2004, I started experiencing abnormal bleeding. At first, I chalked it up to stress or hormonal changes. But as the weeks turned into months, the bleeding intensified. I felt as though my body was crying out for help, but the answers were nowhere to be found.

Alongside the bleeding, I began to experience persistent hip and lower back pain that refused to subside. It was a dull, nagging ache at first, but over time it became more intense, making even simple movements uncomfortable. These physical symptoms combined with the emotional toll of my marriage left me feeling trapped in a body and life that seemed to be working against me.

I visited doctor after doctor, enduring countless tests, only to be met with inconclusive results. The specialists discovered small fibroid cysts but dismissed them as insignificant, telling me they

couldn't possibly be the cause of such severe symptoms. But deep down, I knew something was terribly wrong.

For two long years, I was shuffled between medical professionals who seemed more puzzled than concerned. Meanwhile, the bleeding became constant, dictating every aspect of my life. I couldn't sleep through the night without waking up dizzy and weak. Even the simplest tasks, like standing up too quickly, left me lightheaded. My life began to revolve around managing my symptoms, and my fear grew with every passing day.

One night, the unthinkable happened. I got up in the middle of the night to use the bathroom, and as soon as I stood, everything went black. When I regained consciousness, I was lying on the cold bathroom floor. My head throbbed, my body felt lifeless, and I was overcome with terror. I knew this was not just exhaustion or stress—something far more serious was at play.

That night, my mom happened to be staying over, which turned out to be a blessing I didn't fully realize until later. My husband was upstairs with me when I fainted, and he found me lying on the bathroom floor, barely conscious. Meanwhile, my mom was downstairs, while our three children, who were just 9, 7, and 3 years old slept. Had she not been there that night, he likely would have been downstairs watching TV, oblivious to what was happening, and I might have been left lying there, unheard and unnoticed. Instead, he was able to rush me to the hospital while my mom stayed behind to care for the children. At the hospital, the severity of my condition became clear: my hemoglobin levels had plummeted to 5, a dangerously low level compared to the normal range of 12 to 16. The doctors explained that my blood loss was life threatening and that I needed immediate intervention to save my life.

After a series of blood tests, ultrasounds, MRIs and a PET scan, the truth was finally revealed: I had Stage 3B Cervical Cancer. The bleeding was caused by a tumor that had grown behind my cervix and into my pelvic region. It had been hiding in plain sight, evading detection in my earlier tests and pap smears.

Due to the advanced stage of the cancer, the doctors told me I likely had only two years to live. Hearing those words felt like time itself had stopped. Two years. Just 24 months. How do you measure a life in such a short span? My mind raced with questions and fears—questions the

doctors couldn't answer and fears I couldn't silence. I thought of my children. Would they even remember me? Who would comfort them when they cried, cheer them on in school plays, or guide them through life's challenges?

The weight of that prognosis was suffocating. I imagined all the moments I would miss—the birthdays, the milestones, the everyday joys of watching them grow up. My heart broke at the thought of my youngest, who might barely remember the sound of my voice or the feel of my hugs.

I wasn't just scared; I was angry. I had always done everything right. I kept up with my checkups, had normal pap smears, and lived a healthy lifestyle. How could this be happening? How could my life be reduced to a mere two years, a deadline hanging over me like a ticking clock?

But amid the despair, something else stirred deep within me—a fierce, almost primal determination. Two years might be what they gave me, but I was not going to let cancer dictate the rest of my life. I refused to accept that this disease would rob my children of their mother. If I had to fight tooth and nail, I would do it—not just for myself, but for them. My children deserved a mother who fought to stay by their side.

Those words, "two years to live," could have been a death sentence, but I chose to see them as a challenge. They lit a fire within me, one that would carry me through the darkest and most grueling days ahead. I wasn't ready to give up, not then, not ever.

The following days were a whirlwind of decisions and treatment plans. I was referred to a radiation oncologist who outlined an aggressive regimen: five and a half weeks of daily radiation and chemotherapy. The goal was to shrink the tumor and stop its spread.

The treatments were brutal. Each session of radiation felt like it was burning me from the inside out, leaving me nauseous and drained. Chemotherapy added another layer of misery—constant fatigue, hair loss, and a sense of fragility I had never experienced before. My body was ravaged, but my spirit refused to break. My children needed me, and that thought became my anchor.

Even with aggressive treatment, the tumor only shrank by half. High-dose internal radiation was the next step, a procedure that was as painful as it was necessary. I endured three rounds, each one leaving me physically and emotionally shattered. Radiation didn't just target cancer; it destroyed healthy tissues and organs, leaving me with severe complications that I would battle for years to come.

During this grueling period, I experienced a moment of clarity that would change the course of my life. Laying on a table in the radiation room, I had a sudden realization: *I want to help women take care of themselves.* It was a simple thought but profoundly transformative. My suffering began to take on a purpose. I wanted to ensure that no other woman would ignore her body's cries for help or put herself last in the name of being a caregiver.

After four months of intense treatments, I emerged from treatment cancer-free. The tumor was gone, but the journey was far from over. Radiation had left me with permanent damage, requiring 11 major surgeries and countless smaller procedures. My digestive system was compromised, and the physical scars were matched only by the emotional ones.

Surviving cancer gave me the strength to confront another battle—my toxic marriage. My husband's behavior during my illness had confirmed what I already knew: I deserved better. The man who should have been my rock was instead my tormentor, dismissing my pain and belittling my struggles. For years, I had stayed out of fear—fear of financial instability, fear of judgment, fear of the unknown. But surviving cancer taught me that life is too precious to waste in unhappiness.

Leaving my marriage was one of the hardest decisions I've ever made, but it was also the most liberating. It marked the beginning of a new chapter, one where I could focus on healing and rediscovering myself. I wanted more than just survival—I wanted to thrive.

With my newfound freedom, I turned my focus to my passion for health and wellness. My own journey had revealed the critical importance of self-care, and I felt compelled to share that message with other women. Determined to make a difference, I became a Functional Nutritional Health Coach, enrolling in a program that gave me the tools to guide women through their own transformations.

Once I balanced my body, everything changed. I lost weight and have kept it off, my skin became clearer and more radiant, I started sleeping better, my mindset improved, and I felt better than I had in years. These changes were life-altering, and they reinforced just how powerful proper nutrition, self-care, and a holistic approach to health can be. Now, I use my experience to help other women discover their own potential for healing, growth, and transformation.

As I delved deeper into the connection between nutrition and healing, I expanded my expertise, becoming a Nutritional Therapist and a Culinary Nutrition Expert. I discovered the incredible power of food to heal the body, a lesson I applied not only to my own recovery but also to the lives of hundreds of women I've had the privilege to help. Through this knowledge, I've empowered women to reclaim their health, proving that transformation is possible when we nourish ourselves—mind, body, and soul.

When your body is balanced, everything changes. Weight comes off naturally, you enjoy better sleep, moods stabilize, your skin glows, and you feel your best. Unfortunately, so many women settle for pain and discomfort because they've forgotten what it feels like to truly feel good. That's where I come in—to help women rediscover their vitality and teach them that they don't have to live in a constant state of exhaustion, pain, or dissatisfaction. Together, we create a path to healing and transformation, reminding women that they are worth the effort.

Today, I offer three and six-month personalized programs that helps women reclaim their health, change their mindset, and take back their lives. My work is deeply personal, rooted in the lessons I learned through my journey. I teach women that self-care is not selfish, that their bodies are always communicating with them, and that resilience is a skill that can be nurtured.

Nineteen years have passed since my cancer diagnosis, and I have been cancer-free ever since. My body bears the scars of my battle—physical reminders of the war I waged—but each one is a testament to my strength, determination, and the unyielding will to survive. These years have been filled with milestones I once feared I might never see, moments that make every struggle, every tear, and every challenge worth it.

I've had the privilege of watching my children grow into incredible adults, cheering them on every step of the way. From their countless sporting events to their school achievements, I've celebrated their challenges, milestones, and accomplishments with immense pride. I was there, cheering from the sidelines, watching them give their all on the field, pushing through obstacles, and rising to every occasion. I've seen them graduate from high school and college, take on new challenges, and embrace the careers and lives they've worked so hard to build. Every victory, big or small, has been a moment to celebrate their growth and determination, and I couldn't be prouder of the paths they've chosen.

Today, my oldest, now 28, is engaged to be married, and I'm filled with joy as he enters this beautiful new chapter in his life. My middle child, 25, is married and expecting her first child, giving me the indescribable honor of becoming a grandmother. My youngest, 21, is chasing his entrepreneurial dreams and is well on his way to starting a business he's passionate about.

These moments—moments I once thought I might miss—are the treasures of my life. They are the reasons I fought so hard to stay, the proof that my determination was not in vain. Watching my children thrive, love, and pursue their dreams is the greatest reward of all. It's a reminder that no matter how dark the journey may seem, there is always light waiting on the other side. For that, I am endlessly grateful.

As I reflect on my journey, I am filled with gratitude—not just for my survival but for the opportunity to turn my pain into purpose. My story is one of rising, leading, and living—a testament to the power of resilience, courage, and self-love. It is proof that no matter how dire the circumstances, it's never too late to prioritize yourself, make a change, and rise above adversity. I've been where so many women find themselves: overwhelmed, undervalued, and unsure of how to move forward.

By sharing my story, I hope to inspire other women to take control of their health and their lives. Life may knock us down, but we always have the strength within us to rise.

THINGS I HAVE LEARNED

Personal Experience as a Catalyst for Coaching

1. **Surviving and Thriving After Adversity**: My battle with cancer, toxic relationships, and the subsequent transformation has given me first-hand experience of what it means to overcome seemingly insurmountable obstacles.
2. **Learning to Listen to Your Body**: My health crisis taught me the importance of prioritizing and listening to my body—a lesson many women neglect due to societal pressures.
3. **Healing the Whole Self**: Navigating the emotional toll of illness and an unhealthy marriage has equipped me to address both the physical and emotional aspects of health, ensuring a holistic approach in my coaching practice.

VALUABLE LESSONS LEARNED

1. **Self-Care is Non-Negotiable**: Ignoring my own needs for too long resulted in a life threatening situation. This hard-learned lesson emphasizes the importance of self-care, which I now instill in my clients.
2. **Strength is Found in Vulnerability**: By sharing my story openly, I have turned vulnerability into empowerment—both for myself and those I coach.
3. **Mindset Shapes Outcomes**: Shifting from victimhood to empowerment allows me to reclaim my life, and now I help others do the same by fostering resilience and positive mindsets.
4. **Transformation is Possible at Any Stage**: My personal evolution shows that no matter how dire a situation seems, meaningful change is possible when one takes ownership of their health and life.

CORE MESSAGES TO READERS

- **Put Yourself First**: Women must embrace the idea that self-care is not selfish but necessary.
- **Listen to Your Body**: Ignoring physical symptoms or gut feelings can have severe consequences.
- **Prioritize Health and Wellness**: Investing in oneself is the foundation for thriving in all areas of life.
- **Resilience is Within Us All**: Obstacles are steppingstones to transformation when approached with courage and support.

HOW I HOPE TO INSPIRE CHANGE

- **Empowerment Through Connection:** By sharing my struggles and triumphs, I hope to help readers feel seen, understood, and validated. I want them to recognize that they are not alone in their challenges and to feel empowered to take charge of their health and lives.
- **Prioritizing Health and Wellness:** One of the key messages of my journey is the importance of making health and wellness a priority. It's not just about survival—it's about thriving. I want readers to understand that their well-being matters and that investing in themselves is the foundation for a better, more fulfilling life.
- **Actionable Steps for Change:** My story is more than just inspiration—it's a practical guide. I aim to motivate readers to prioritize their physical, emotional, and mental health by embracing healthier habits, listening to their bodies, and seeking the right support to help them achieve their goals. Whether that support comes from trusted resources, loved ones, or a knowledgeable health coach, having guidance on the journey can make all the difference in creating lasting change.
- **A Beacon of Hope:** My journey from adversity to transformation demonstrates that no matter how dire the circumstances, there

is always a path forward. By prioritizing health, building resilience, and taking actionable steps, anyone can overcome obstacles and create a life of strength and purpose.

PERSONAL AND PROFESSIONAL ALIGNMENT

The themes of *She Rises, She Leads, She Lives* resonate deeply with my mission.

- **Rising**: I have risen from the ashes of adversity and help other women rise from theirs, whether it's illness, self-doubt, or toxic situations.
- **Leading**: Through my Nutritional Health Coaching, I lead women to rediscover their power and take charge of their well-being.
- **Living**: I embody the idea of thriving after hardship, offering hope that life can be fulfilling, joyful, and purposeful.
- **Professional Validation**: My story sets me apart as someone who has walked the walk.
- **Guiding women through their own journeys** has become my mission. My 3 and 6- month personalized programs are a direct extension of the lessons I've learned and shared in my story—providing structure, support, and strategies to help women transform their lives and take back control of their health and happiness.
- **Fulfillment in Personal Life**: Coaching allows me to live in alignment with my values, continue my healing journey, and inspire my children and others by leading a life of purpose, resilience, and empowerment.

Kerrie D. Stone

Founder of SheThatExists
Minister, Metaphysician, Mystical Life Coach,
Visionary & Creative Director

https://www.linkedin.com/in/rev-kerrie-d-stone-a19964299/
https://www.facebook.com/shethatexists
https://www.instagram.com/shethatexiststheuniteroftribes/
https://shethatexists.com/
https://kerriedstone.com/

Kerrie D. Stone, Founder of SheThatExists, is a former child performer in dance/theater performance arts at Story Book Theater Playhouse in Texas. She is a former gymnast and has performed in parades. A former select corporate softball athlete, she has played several team sports. She is a musician trained in clarinet, piano, and the xylophone, having performed in concert and jazz bands. She is an awarded esthetician. A former showwoman, she produced her own community show as a single mom. Born a spiritual child, she professed her faith in Creator at age 15. A champion in supporting others in their greatness, she has 36 years of team/leadership experience. Today she is an Ordained Minister in service of life as sacred, a mystical life coach, metaphysician, visionary, wisdom teacher, polymath, Creative Director, and Comedian. Her favorite passion is being momma. She is earning her Masters degree and is a PhD candidate.

Be the Lighthouse.
Be a Wayshower.
Rise. Lead. Live.

By Kerrie D. Stone

Whatever comes your way in life, keep going.

Whatever life throws at you, hide in the secret place deep inside of your heart and refuse to disconnect from your Self as a living, breathing soul.

When the opposing forces come to us to destroy our dreams, our lives, our family, our children, and to test our ability to master inner peace, know that nothing outside of us can overcome us.

Life is always going to bring things our way to force us to grow mentally, emotionally, and spiritually.

When life seems lonely, and no one seems to care, please know that you are never alone.

Creator is within us and Creator loves us.

We have tests in life so that we can have a testimony.

You can rise above every single challenge that life throws at you.

It may not seem like we can go on. It may seem like our lives and hearts are shattered into a million pieces and that our souls have been shattered across all time, space, and the entire universe. This may even be true, however, know that you can recover all of you and that nothing is permanent. The Creator can send strangers to show up for you; please be open to receiving every single miracle that life has for you. Do not give up on your life or your purpose and reason for being born on this Earth.

Some things in life happen to us that we never would have ever expected.

There are times that you will feel like you are completely in the dark.

There are times when it feels like the whole world is against us, and even our family members and those who are supposed to love us, protect us, and cherish us turn against us.

Then, there are other times that you will feel like you have lost your spark of life within.

There are going to be days when you don't want to wake up and face life.

There are going to be days when it feels so dark that you will never see the light ever again.

There are going to be days where it feels like that pain inside and the unknown fears that try to consume us are never going to go away.

There are going to be times in your life when you feel completely overwhelmed, completely consumed, abandoned, and you feel like giving in.

There are going to be days when you feel that you are going to lose it all and that everything that you worked so hard for is going to disappear, and you are going to lose it all or even be homeless or without shelter.

During these times of pain, grief, unexpected loss, war on our lives, darkness, and uncertainty where we don't feel like there is a way out or that we will survive, that is the time to rest, relax, go deep within our hearts, be extremely present with our lives, get quiet and go within, and go deep into your body temple and connect to Creator within as living breathing soul and allow Creator's light within you to dissolve every single fear of the unknown of the future. This is the time to be still and know that Creator is in control and that all is well. This is the time to be still and quiet and go within and be completely present with our breath.

Our breath is the breath of the living God who lives within us. We must get really comfortable with being still and going into our body temple and connecting to God within. Connecting to our breath which is the living breath of God/Life/Creator is an absolute, essential resource that we have for sustainability and growth in life.

The only way out is within. We have to be our own best friend. We have to know how to stay dedicated to our Self, close to Creator within, believe in our Self, and live in our hearts and stay connected to our breath which is Creator's breath living within us.

During these times, this is the time to feel our pain all the way through. This is the time to cry and feel every emotion on the spectrum ALL the WAY through. This is not the time to hide the pain with drugs, mindless television, social media scrolling, or alcohol. This is not the time to pretend to be "busy" or to disassociate your self by numbing your self. This is the time to feel the pain all the way through. This is the time to allow the fires of life to burn within you and to refine you. This is the time to allow the pain inside of your heart to lead you to the heart of the matter, the true depths of your being as soul, and to allow your Self to go deeper within your body temple and heart as soul and connect deeper to your spirit than ever before. This is where you will find Creator Almighty within and connect to your own divinity. This is the time to connect to your spiritual and divine nature and get still and quiet and listen to the truth of the still, small voice of Creator within you. This is the time to lie down and rest: to be still and allow your world to fall apart so everything can come together for the greater good of your life.

I want to say that during these moments of going within, it is ok to allow your Self to die. To die to the old patterns and old ways that no longer serve you. To die to the patterns of avoidance, disassociating, staying busy, numbing, living in fear, or doubt, dwelling in past disappointments, and living in denial simply to stay alive.

Allow your Self to feel everything that you have been avoiding feeling. Feel all of your feels deep inside your body temple, knowing that it is safe to feel and stay inside of your body temple, feeling all of your fears completely until they all subside. All truth and all answers lie within us. Creator Almighty is within. Creator is love. It is ALL an inside journey. Love your Self divinely through every single storm of life, through all adversity, and through every single area of life where you have felt abandoned, betrayed, or ashamed. Surrender inside of your body temple to the love that is within you and the love that is you. Learn how to nurture your Self like never before. Feel every emotion and feeling all the way through. Do not deny your Self this experience because this is essential to your mental, emotional, and spiritual growth. We come into this life to grow mentally, emotionally, and spiritually.

This is the greatest space to be in—our body temple—fully surrendered to our Maker and still. Be still and know that God is God. After you allow your Self to feel everything you have been avoiding to feel and after allowing your Self to die to all the lies, illusions, and thoughts of being separate from all of life and creation and your divinity within, this form of death will give you the ability to rise. Growth hurts. It is a dying process. Dying to the old, worn-out ways and cycles that no longer serve us. It hurts to be a witness of our own spiritual death process, however, when we die to our old thoughts that do not serve us, then we can take on new thought forms and new ways of being that do serve our greater good. God wants to work things out for our good. According to Romans 8:28, God is always working out things for our good as we are focusing on our higher calling and our purposes that our Maker has for us. We are all being called according to our Maker's purposes, and it's a deep dive, and the only way out is in.

I know this because the unexpected things in life that happened to me, I thought, were going to be the death of me. When I allowed my Self to die this form of spiritual death, the darkness became light, and the new light that came in provided new awareness that I did not even know existed. After my spiritual death, I realized that through anything, I can continue to rise. I can die spiritually to old ways that no longer serve me, and I can continue to rise every single time. I've learned that as long as we stay in our hearts and allow our Selves to feel and cry and stay connected to Creator, close to Creator within us, and spend time inside of our body temple to recover our spirit and just be alone in our body temple with Creator, connecting to our own divinity within, we can renew our spirit, and tap into greater wisdom than we even knew existed. We can die and rise like the phoenix for real. Resting our minds, hearts, bodies, and spirits is truly an essential life skill. I see so many people struggling with life and their personal growth simply because they get addicted to the outer chaos and stay in "busy mode". They refuse to get still and do what I call "Inner Body Temple Stillness Practices". We have to get still and go within the body temple in order to grow mentally, emotionally, and spiritually. Our Creator wants us to grow and evolve. We came here to learn, evolve, and grow mentally, emotionally, and spiritually, not just physically.

Everything is possible, and this life is truly a mystery.

We can not explain the Sovereignty of our Maker, and life truly is a mystery that we just need to surrender to and sit back and enjoy the ride. Life is truly a journey. No one taught me this or told me this growing up. I did not learn about this until well into my 30s.

When we are able to overcome all of the darkness, all of the unknowns, all of the fear, doubt, unnecessary worry, and pain, we are able to lead and guide with assurance and knowing that it is more than safe to share our voice, stand in our truth and knowing and receive even greater direction by going within our body temple and connecting to Creator within for our lives. When we spend time within our body temple and come to know our Self as soul and our oneness with Creation, we connect with our true power, what I like to call our Inner Guidance

System. Our Inner Guidance System will guide us, we will know because we will feel the impetus within. Some people call this our Intuition. It is gifted to us by our Maker. Going within guides us and helps us understand our path going forward in life. It is important to not stay stuck. It's also important not to look back when we have crossed paths with others who did not have the best intentions for us.

When it comes to leadership, we must continually keep moving forward, encouraging our Selves and being confident in our path. Once we have overcome any form of adversity and life-threatening challenge, then we will come deeper into our gift of leadership. A true leader trust their intuition. A true leader will always listen to the still, small voice within. A true leader will never follow the crowd. A true leader lives set apart. I have been living set apart since about 2015 after creating, directing, organizing, envisioning, and producing a live community show that was gifted to me by Creator. I was able to see the world for what it actually is through that life experience. I was gifted the wisdom and the knowledge to live set apart.

Life will gift us with situations or experiences that may be hard or challenging; however, it is for our greater good and for us to learn great wisdom. A true leader listens to Creator within. A true leader will not listen to man-made things, as the Word says that those who put their faith or trust in men are cursed. A true leader will have impeccable character and ethics. A true leader will keep their standards very high and not do something just because other people are doing it. As a leader, I do not follow the blind. As a leader, I do not follow trends. I get all of my guidance and direction from within. I pay attention to leadership styles that are ancient and that have worked for over 1,500 years. A true leader does not fold just because of the crowd or because of others who appear to have a greater influence. A true leader does not fold under pressure. A true leader will not quit just because they have opponents who criticize, mock them, or attempt to destroy them, slander them, betray them, and take them down. A true leader will not quit. A true leader will stand and voice the truth. A true leader does not have to fight because a true leader knows that, according to Exodus 14:14, it is Creator who fights our battles for us. As a true leader, I receive the vision from Creator, and I stand and see it through until the mission is complete. Sometimes, this may take a lifetime, however, we must persist, endure, and be patient. We must learn how to wait on God's divine timing in all things.

There is going to be opposition when you are leading. There is always going to be darkness that tries to come in and overtake. The battle does not belong to you; it belongs to Creator. A true leader will have tests and trials, and they will have the biggest obstacles inside of their own family tree. I know this because I have experienced this, and I am currently enduring and trusting Creator my Self for my life and family tree. A true leader will always equip, inspire, empower, and educate others to the best of their ability. As a true leader, we serve. We serve in our hearts, we show this in how we are called to show up. We serve by showing others the love of Creator, even when it hurts. As a true leader, we have to make critical decisions. We do this by shutting out all of the outside noise and connecting to Creator within for guidance.

This is why the signature SheThatExists Inner Body Temple Stillness Practices that I teach are essential for any type of personal or spiritual growth and development. A true leader knows that true responsibility is responding to your soul's purpose and calling. True responsibility is going in and shutting out the outside noise and chaos, connecting with Creator within, and taking the highest aligned action steps that our Maker calls us to take whether we understand it or not. Most of the world will not understand. Many of our friends and family members will not understand.

As a leader, we must learn to be good stewards of everything we have in our lives. As a leader, we must always be clear in our hearts, pray to

Creator, and let go of the old wounds of the past. We must keep our hearts pure. We must keep trusting all of the good that our Maker has for us and continue this path, even when it seems that the road is unclear, or that it is over, that " all is lost", and that it is the end of the road for us. As leaders, we must persevere. As leaders, we must stay the course. As leaders, we must know that opposition and seeming evil will appear in our lives, but the light of Creator within us will not allow the evil to overtake us. As leaders, there will be many sent to disparage us, and there will even be people sent to try to defame us and destroy our character. A true leader will never let anyone or the world turn them against their true Self. My identity is as a child of Creator, and my Master teacher and Lord is Yahushua. I Am a Mystic. This means that I know my Maker is within. The Kingdom of Heaven is within you. Luke 17:21

Remember, there are always going to be storms, trials, and tribulations in life.

Remember the truth that when your parents forsake and abandon you that it is the Creator who takes us in. I know this because I have lived this truth.

Grace is real. Grace is very deep in the Hebrew language. In the Hebrew language it is a place where our Maker provides protection, sustainability, and provision for life. Grace is a camp, a graceful precious place of healing, strength, salvation, and rescue.

We are born to discover our treasure that is hidden deep within underneath all of the pain, personal trials, broken hearts, sorrow, unknown fears, grief, loss, and emotional heartache.

It is my prayer that anyone reading this will discover the hidden treasures within themselves. The true treasure that we seek is not riches, fame, being popular, having a boyfriend/girlfriend, having a large number of social media followers/fans—no! The true treasure that you seek is always found deep within the Self. Conquer your fears! Face your obstacles! Thrive against all odds. Discover or rediscover your Self. Victory forged through hardship can be the most valuable reward of all. Creator works in mysterious ways and supplies all of our needs according to His riches and glory.

Never give up. Choose perseverance. Choose you.

Every day you wake up, know that Creator's mercy and grace are real and that you can always rewrite your story.

Conquer your inner fears and find the wealth of hidden treasure that is within.

If you have children, they will honor you for staying true to your Self as soul.

They may not see you in the beginning; however, before it's all over with, they will see that you stayed true and did not allow your Self to be deceived by outside illusions—they will know that Creator is real and is within because of your dedication, resilience, and fortitude. This is the best way that you can lead and live by example.

They will see you and recognize you for your endurance, dignity, resilience, perseverance, and strength.

If the trees can stand strong despite all the storms of life, so can we.

Reignite your dreams.

Allow the spirit of resilience to embody you.

Do not listen to the world or naysayers.

Allow hope to come alive inside of you.

Allow the seeds of the amazing potential that Creator placed within you to flourish by watering and nurturing your Self. Give your Self sunshine and water. We are living trees. Remember to breathe deep from your belly.

WE become heroes from the spirit of resilience that we discover within.

We are called to overcome and live victoriously. Our Maker loves us. Our Maker has us at all times when we trust the journey from within, go deep, and allow our Selves to grow from within. Let go of the resistance. We are loved by our Creator. We can overcome all things. Know you are loved with the greatest and purest of love by Creator. Creator will always come through on time. Allow Creator's love in no matter how much the pain wants to consume and overtake you.

Now promise me to live.

Promise me to choose life.

Promise me to endure.

Promise me to keep the faith at all times.

Rest as long as you need to. It's safe to rest peacefully.

Rise when you are ready.

Lead with a WHOLE heart.

Live fully.

Take this wisdom that I am sharing and BE the LIGHTHOUSE.

We are called to be the light of the world and the salt of the Earth.

The World needs you.

We are living in auspicious times.

Respond to Creator's calling over your life.

Creator will qualify you when you are being called.

Surrender to your higher calling and your soul's true purpose/calling.

It is never too late.

Trust your Self. Trust Creator.

God never fails.

You will know this is for you because you will feel the resonance deep inside.

In Honor of All of Life as Sacred,
Reverend Kerrie D. Stone

JOIN THE MOVEMENT!
#BAUW

Becoming An Unstoppable Woman
With She Rises Studios

She Rises Studios was founded by Hanna Olivas and Adriana Luna Carlos, the mother-daughter duo, in mid-2020 as they saw a need to help empower women worldwide. They are the podcast hosts of the *She Rises Studios Podcast* and Amazon best-selling authors and motivational speakers who travel the world. Hanna and Adriana are the movement creators of #BAUW - Becoming An Unstoppable Woman: The movement has been created to universally impact women of all ages, at whatever stage of life, to overcome insecurities, and adversities, and develop an unstoppable mindset. She Rises Studios educates, celebrates, and empowers women globally.

Looking to Join Us in our Next Anthology or Publish YOUR Own?

She Rises Studios Publishing offers full-service publishing, marketing, book tour, and campaign services. For more information, contact info@sherisesstudios.com

We are always looking for women who want to share their stories and expertise and feature their businesses on our podcasts, in our books, and in our magazines.

SEE WHAT WE DO

OUR PODCAST

OUR BOOKS

OUR SERVICES

Be featured in the Becoming An Unstoppable Woman magazine, published in 13 countries and sold in all major retailers. Get the visibility you need to LEVEL UP in your business!

Have your own TV show streamed across major platforms like Roku TV, Amazon Fire Stick, Apple TV and more!

Learn to leverage your expertise. Build your online presence and grow your audience with FENIX TV.
https://fenixtv.sherisesstudios.com/

Visit www.SheRisesStudios.com to see how YOU can join the #BAUW movement and help your community to achieve the UNSTOPPABLE mindset.

Have you checked out the *She Rises Studios Podcast?*

Find us on all MAJOR platforms: Spotify, IHeartRadio, Apple Podcasts, Google Podcasts, etc.

Looking to become a sponsor or build a partnership?

Email us at info@sherisesstudios.com